Stories for the Family's Heart

Stories for the Family's Heart

Over 100 Stories to Encourage Your Family

COMPILED BY ALICE GRAY

Multnomah Publishers *Sisters, Oregon*

Every effort has been made to provide proper and accurate source attribution for selections in this volume. Should any attribution be found to be incorrect, the publisher welcomes written documentation supporting correction for subsequent printings. For material not in the public domain, selections were made according to generally accepted fair-use standards and practices. The publisher gratefully acknowledges the cooperation of publishers and individuals granting permission for use of longer selections; please see the bibliography for full attribution of these sources.

STORIES FOR THE FAMILY'S HEART
published by Multnomah Publishers, Inc.

© 1998 by Multnomah Publishers, Inc.

International Standard Book Number: 1-57673-356-4

Cover art by Donna Green
Design by Kevin Keller

Printed in the United States of America

Unless otherwise indicated, Scripture quotations are from
The Holy Bible, New International Version (NIV) © 1973, 1984 by International
Bible Society, used by permission of Zondervan Publishing House

Also quoted The Holy Bible, King James Version (KJV)

Multnomah is a trademark of Multnomah Publishers and is registered with the
U.S. Trademark and Patent Office.
The colophon is a trademark of Multnomah Publishers, Inc.

For information:
MULTNOMAH PUBLISHERS, INC.•POST OFFICE BOX 1720•SISTERS, OREGON 97759

Library of Congress Cataloging–in–Publication Data
Stories for the Family's heart/ [compiled] by Alice Gray.
     p. cm.   Includes bibliographical references (p.).   ISBN 1-57673-356-4
     1. Family—Anecdotes. 2. Conduct of life—Anecdotes. I. Gray, Alice, 1939–
HQ734.S9 1998
306.85—dc21   98–23521
                                                                              CIP

98 99 00 01 02 03 04 05 — 10 9 8 7 6 5 4 3 2

To Breanah—
We will cuddle up beside the fireplace
with popcorn, pillows and books
and read into the night
until we both fall fast asleep.

Grandma loves you, precious one.

Other books compiled by Alice Gray

Stories for the Heart
More Stories for the Heart
Christmas Stories for the Heart
Keepsakes for the Heart—Mothers
Keepsakes for the Heart—Friendship

(Keepsakes for the Heart are uniquely designed treasure boxes with postcards and a small book tucked inside.)

A special thank you—

To Doreen Button, Ruth King, Nancy Larson,
Casandra Lindell, Sandra Snavely, and Becky Wilkins
who helped me choose these wonderful stories.

To readers from all over the world
who encouraged me through letters and stories...
I wish we could meet face to face.
Perhaps someday we will.

To Kerri Loesche
who masterfully directed all the details.

To Al Gray
whose thoughtful ways have endured through all the years.

To friends and family
who have cheered me on.

Together we all did it!
Let's celebrate with long walks, warms hugs, and chocolate.

Other books compiled by Alice Gray

Stories for the Heart
More Stories for the Heart
Christmas Stories for the Heart
Keepsakes for the Heart—Mothers
Keepsakes for the Heart—Friendship

*(Keepsakes for the Heart are uniquely designed treasure boxes
with postcards and a small book tucked inside. Available Fall 1998.)*

Contents

Compassion

LOOK ALIKES

While working at a medical center, I noticed a distinguished gentleman and his young son on their daily visits to the chemotherapy center. Impeccably tailored suit and a head of lush salt-and-pepper hair made the man stand out. As I admired him and his smiling five-year-old, I found it impossible to tell who was receiving treatment.

One day, as they walked past, my attention was drawn to the boy. The cap he usually wore was missing, and I could now see a shiny bald head. I turned toward the father. To my surprise, he was as bald as his son.

"Look at my dad!" the boy said cheerfully. "He shaved his head so we'd look the same. We're going to grow our hair back together!"

His father simply smiled, looking more distinguished than ever.

Linda Mango
Reprinted with permission of
the Reader's Digest Association, Inc.

Ragamuffin Brother

Ron Mehl
from God Works the Night Shift

R oy Angel was a poor preacher with a millionaire brother. It was back in the oil boom days of the late 1940s. Roy's older brother happened to own the right piece of Texas prairie at the right time. When he sold, he became a multimillionaire overnight. Building on that good fortune, the elder Angel made some strategic investments on the stock market, and then cashed in on several mushrooming business enterprises. He moved into the penthouse of a large apartment building in New York City, and managed his investments from a posh Wall Street office.

A week before Christmas one year, the wealthy businessman visited his preacher brother in Chicago, and presented him with a new car—a gleaming, top-of-the-line Packard. Roy always kept his new car down the street in a parking garage, where it would remain under the careful eye of an attendant. That's why he was surprised one morning when he came to get his Packard and saw a young, ragamuffin ghetto boy with his face pressed up against one of the car windows. The little boy wasn't doing anything really suspicious, he was obviously just peering into the new car's interior with wide, admiring eyes.

"Hello, son," Roy said.

The boy looked around at him. "Is this your car, Mister?"

"Yes," Roy replied, "it is."

"How much did it cost?"

"Well, I really don't know how much it cost."

"You mean, you own this car and you don't know how much it cost?"

"No, I don't—because my brother gave it to me. As a present."

At this the boy's eyes grew even wider. He thought about something for a moment and then said wistfully, "I wish...I wish..."

Roy thought he knew how the boy would finish the sentence. He thought he was going to say, *I wish I had a brother like that.*

But he didn't. The boy looked up at Roy and said, "I wish...I wish I could be a brother like that."

That intrigued the minister, and (because these were more innocent times) he said, "Well, son, would you like to take a ride?"

The boy immediately replied, "You bet!"

So they got in the car together, exited the parking garage, and drove slowly down the street. The little boy ran his hand across the soft fabric of the front seat, inhaled the new car smell, and touched the shiny metal of the dashboard. Then he looked at his new friend and said, "Mister, would you—could you—take me by my house? It's just a few blocks from here."

Again, Roy assumed he knew what the lad wanted to do. He thought the boy probably wanted to show off the car he was riding in to some of the neighborhood kids. Well, he thought, why not? So at his young passenger's direction, Roy pulled up in front of an old, run-down tenement building.

"Mister," the boy said as they stopped at the curb, "would you stay here just a minute? I'll be right back!"

Roy let the car idle, as the boy rushed upstairs and disappeared.

After about ten minutes, the preacher began to wonder where the boy had taken himself. He got out of the car and looked up the unlighted stairwell. As he was looking up the dark stairs, he heard someone slowly coming down. The first thing he saw emerging from the gloom were two limp little legs. A moment later, Roy realized it was the little boy carrying a younger boy, evidently his brother.

The boy gently sat his brother down on the curb. "See?" he said with satisfaction, "It's just like I told you. It's a brand new car. His brother gave it to him, and someday, *I'm going to buy you a car just like that!"*

When I heard that story, I was moved by one brother's generosity toward another. But it wasn't the millionaire's gift that impressed me. He, after all, could have purchased his brother a fleet of Packards without even feeling the pinch. No, I found myself moved by the heart desire of the little boy from the slums. Why did he dream of an impossible prosperity? So he could lavish it on his brother!

I wish I could be a brother like that.

Lessons in Baseball

Chick Moorman
from Where the Heart Is

As an 11-year-old, I was addicted to baseball. I listened to baseball games on the radio. I watched them on TV. The books I read were about baseball. I took baseball cards to church in hopes of trading with other baseball card junkies. My fantasies? All about baseball.

I played baseball whenever and wherever I could. I played organized or sandlot. I played catch with my brother, with my father, with friends. If all else failed, I bounced a rubber ball off the porch stairs, imagining all kinds of wonderful things happening to me and my team.

It was with this attitude that I entered the 1956 Little League season. I was a shortstop. Not good, not bad. Just addicted.

Gordon was not addicted. Nor was he good. He moved into our neighborhood that year and signed up to play baseball. The kindest way of describing Gordon's baseball skills is to say that he didn't have any. He couldn't catch. He couldn't hit. He couldn't throw. He couldn't run.

In fact, Gordon was afraid of the ball.

I was relieved when the final selections were made and Gordon was assigned to another team. Everyone had to play at least half of each game, and I couldn't see Gordon improving my team's chances in any way. Too bad for the other team.

After two weeks of practice, Gordon dropped out. My friends on his team laughed when they told me how their coach directed two of the team's better players to walk Gordon into the woods and have a chat with him. "Get lost" was the message that was delivered, and "get lost" was the one that was heard.

Gordon got lost.

That scenario violated my eleven-year-old sense of justice, so I did what any indignant shortstop would do. I tattled. I told my coach the whole story. I shared the episode in full detail, figuring my coach would complain to the Little League office and have Gordon returned to his original team. Justice and my team's chances of winning would both be served.

I was wrong. My coach decided that Gordon needed to be on a team that wanted him—one that treated him with respect, one that gave everyone a fair chance to contribute according to their ability.

Gordon became my team member.

I wish I could say Gordon got the big hit in the big game with two outs in the final inning, but it didn't happen. I don't think Gordon even hit a foul ball the entire season. Baseballs hit in his direction (right field) went over him, by him, through him, or off him.

It wasn't that Gordon didn't get help. The coach gave him extra batting practice and worked with him on his fielding, all without much improvement.

I'm not sure if Gordon learned anything from my coach that year. I know I did. I learned to bunt without tipping off my intention. I learned to tag up on a fly if there were less than two outs. I learned to make a smoother pivot around second base on a double play.

I learned a lot from my coach that summer, but my most important lessons weren't about baseball. They were about character and integrity. I learned that everyone has worth, whether they can hit .300 or .030. I learned that we all have value, whether we can stop the ball or have to turn and chase it. I learned that doing what is right, fair and honorable is more important than winning or losing.

It felt good to be on that team that year. I'm grateful that man was my coach. I was proud to be his shortstop and his son.

JUST BEING THERE

I can remember times as my boys were growing up
when one of them would be very troubled or worried
or had endured a disappointment or hurt.
Sometimes after he was in bed at night,
I'd go and just lie down on the bed beside him.
It's nice if you can think of wise, fatherly words in those moments,
but the words aren't always there.
It was enough just to lie beside my boy and be there with him.

Ron Mehl
from Cure for the Troubled Heart

The Tree Man

James W. H. Tumber

When I press my cheek against the window and melt a spot in the frost, I can see Nick Santos—the Christmas tree man—brushing off trees, turning on colored lights, and brewing cocoa in the shed behind his house.

Our apartment is small, so when I jump out of bed, my dad hears my feet hit the floor. He greets me with a big hug, and we eat breakfast. As we eat he says to me, "Not much of a Christmas this year, with me between jobs and with everything else going on." We both have trouble talking about Mom's death.

"But I've been watching Nick Santos," he says, "and I've been remembering the smell of a tree lot just before Christmas. A smell you never forget. Can't buy us a tree this year, but that doesn't mean we can't get a whiff of the stuff to get us in the mood, to give you something to remember. What do you say we make a social call on Santos, see how business has been?" He winks at me.

When we arrive at the yard, Mr. Santos says, "I've been waiting for you." He hands me a cup of cocoa.

Dad asks about each variety of tree on the lot and where each tree came from. He breathes in deeply, capturing the sharp smell of the trees as if he were reaching for a memory. As we are about to leave, Mr. Santos asks me if I see any trees I like. "Not much time left, you know, being Christmas Eve and all. Plenty of good trees here to pick from."

Before I can explain that we aren't here to buy a tree, Dad clears his throat. "Sorry, Santos, maybe next year."

Then the strangest thing happens. Mr. Santos laughs. He laughs so hard a button pops off his shirt.

"So serious, Mr. Andrews," he says. "It's Christmas Eve. Where's your joy?" He bends down and says to me, "Have you ever wondered what happens to all these trees in a few hours if I don't sell them? Worthless. Too green to burn, too big to leave for the trash collectors." Then he says to Dad, "But you won't see old Nick being so serious about it. No sir! No time for that in this business. By Christmas Eve my trees are worth a great deal more to you than they are to me. So take one. Take it, with all my best wishes."

I carry the top of the tree and Dad carries the bottom, and as we walk we talk. I say if I could have anything for Christmas, it would be a leather basketball, the kind that feels smooth and broken in. Dad says he's had his eye on a pair of work boots in the window at Kelsey's Shoe Shop. We would both like steak for dinner. But we know there will be no presents this Christmas.

We set up the tree, but it looks bare with nothing under it. Dad sees my face and tells me to think about all the people who need more and have less than we do. Later, I go up to my room to read. Through the window I see Nick Santos wrapping presents on the bench in his backyard. I watch as he places what looks like a basketball inside a large box and wraps the box in comic papers. He must have a family somewhere, I think, and this thought makes me happy.

On Christmas morning, much to my surprise, there is a present wrapped in comic papers under our tree.

There is no name on it, but I know it's mine. And I know who brought it. I am about ready to tear into it when my dad walks in, holding a large box wrapped in purple foil paper.

"It's not much," he says as he places it on the floor next to the box wrapped in comic papers. "But I know you'll like it."

The two boxes are exactly the same size and exactly the same weight. And when I shake them, they give the same leathery thump. Mr. Santos has brought me a basketball. But it seems that my dad has, too. I open the present from my father first, and I find the basketball I've always wished for. I am about to cry.

"What's the matter, James?" my dad asks. "Don't you like it?"

"Well, you see...," I say. But I can't tell him what I know. So I say instead, "I just wish you had a present to open."

"Well, I don't see any names on this present wrapped in comics. If it makes you feel better, I'll open it." And before I can stop him, he tears open the present.

"Well, I'll be dipped," he says, pulling a pair of black leather boots from the box. "Now, who did this?" he asks. And for the first time all morning, I have no idea.

After lunch I sneak over to thank Mr. Santos, but he isn't there. It's as if he never was—no trees, no needles, no lights. A note tacked to his door reads, "Went to Miami. Back next year. Merry Christmas! Every day of your life."

He never did come back. Even after I grew up, I looked for him every Christmas when Dad and I got together. I looked for him after I left the city and bought a farm where I raised Christmas trees and five boys of my own. I looked for him whenever I saw someone who needed something I could do without. I looked and looked until I finally realized something: Nick Santos did come back. Every day of my life.

A Candle for Barbara

Phyllis Reynolds Naylor
from Christmas through the Years

As usual, Helen Roberts sensed, rather than saw, that Barbara Duffey was waiting for her attention. But Peter, who had put his left boot on his right foot, was prancing around the room and distracting the other children of the fourth grade from the task of putting on their own coats and galoshes.

Helen tried hard to control her impatience. She did want to keep the atmosphere cheerful even in the last turbulent two minutes before the Christmas holiday, but she was eager to get home to her own family.

Peter gave her an impish grin, kicked vigorously, and sent the boot sailing dangerously near a windowpane. The near miss had a generally sobering effect, and Helen turned toward the little girl waiting near her desk.

Barbara the barbarian, one of the more precocious children had dubbed her almost the first day she came to school. Barbara's dresses were always stained with dirt and food, her hair always matted and uncombed. Her shabby shoes, much too big for her, were obviously hand-me-downs.

Helen had wondered more than once about Fred Duffey, knowing vaguely that he cleaned stables at racetracks, moving from state to state as his work required, dragging his uncared-for and apparently unloved little daughter with him.

"What is it, Barbara?" Helen asked, trying hard not to think what the child's Christmas would be like.

"My dad sent you a note. I forgot to give it to you sooner."

Unfolding the crumpled scrap of paper, Helen read the

penciled scrawl: "I will be gone two weeks and it's vacation so my girl will be by herself. Can you take her to the Children's Home after school today—it's so far to walk and she lost her boots."

"Do you know what this note says?" Helen asked.

Barbara nodded with complete unconcern.

"Have you been to the Home before?"

Barbara nodded again. "If you drop me off at the corner by the statue, I could walk the rest."

The room was empty now except for the girl and her teacher. As Barbara began to assemble her scattered crayons, Helen stood staring down at her desk. Could Fred Duffey have cunningly foreseen how she would react to his daughter's situation? Or did he actually think a teacher could callously drop his child at the Children's Home a few days before Christmas?

Then she faced the real questions. Did she dare take Barbara into the intimacy of her home for two weeks? How would her children feel about having a dirty, sullen little stranger intrude upon the happiest time of their year? What would Wallace say if she did bring Barbara home? What would he say if she didn't?

She closed her desk drawer with a bang and gave Barbara a sudden smile. "How would you like to spend Christmas at our house?"

Barbara bent to pick up a crayon, and Helen could not see her face, but her voice was flat as ever. "It don't make no difference. I could walk from the statue."

Helen tried again, lying valiantly: "We'd like very much to have you come, Barbara. I think you'd have a lot of fun with Susan and Mike. They're a little younger than you are, but you could have fun together anyway!"

Still stuffing broken crayons into the box, Barbara seemed only to have half-heard. "Okay," she said at last. "But you better call Mrs. Cary—that's our landlady—and tell her. The Home always does when I get there."

All the way home, Barbara sat silently with her arms clasped tightly around the paper bag with the clothing she'd brought to school that morning. A pitiful lot, Helen thought, to last a child for two weeks.

In the carport, she could hear the sound of feet thudding inside the house as Mike and Susan raced to meet her at the kitchen door. At the sight of Barbara, their mouths dropped wide, and Helen spoke quickly. "Guess what? I've brought Barbara and she's going to stay with us for two whole weeks!"

Then, as Wallace came into the kitchen with the remains of a broken ornament in the dustpan, "This is Mr. Roberts, my husband, Barbara. Barbara's father had to go out of town, Wallace, so I invited her to spend the Christmas vacation with us."

Husband looked at wife, piecing together in a flash the fragments she'd given him in the past about this pupil—the girl who didn't know how to use a handkerchief; the girl who went for a week with a broken finger before someone discovered it; the girl who squirmed uncomfortably when Helen once called her "dear."

"Well," he said slowly, "we'll really have a good time this year, won't we, kids?" Then he looked back to Helen. "It's time we did some sharing."

And share they did—doggedly, day after day. Even the children shared from the outset without too much coaching. After supper, Mike got out his checkerboard and asked Barbara to play, but she shook her head indifferently and tried to efface herself even more among the pillows on the couch.

In place of the usual bedtime story, Helen got out the portfolio of Nativity pictures she'd collected through the years, and for the first time Barbara's face took on some expression. When Helen, holding the pictures up one by one, came to "The Gift of the Magi," Barbara said with sudden decision and intensity, "I like that the best. I wish my dad could see it."

"Then take it home with you," Helen said. "I can easily get another for us." But as she handed over the picture, she could not help wondering what Fred Duffey would say when presented with it—or whether he'd say anything at all.

So the sharing went on. Wallace even took pains to work the little guest into all the family shots he took of the tree at various stages of its decoration, the hanging of the stockings on Christmas Eve, the opening of the presents on Christmas morning. And Barbara seemed to have as many packages as Susan and Mike. "Santa" had left her a new bracelet and necklace set, a jeweled hairbrush and a music box. With bright wrappings, Helen and Susan had made used clothing donated by neighbors seem almost like new gifts. Barbara, however, opened the gifts methodically and set them aside as though they did not really belong to her. Helen could only shake her head in bewilderment.

There was turkey for dinner and candymaking in the afternoon. Then, after the sun had set, the family went through a little ceremony that was uniquely theirs and which the children seemed to cherish—perhaps because Mike had first proposed it. Where he'd picked up the idea puzzled Helen, but Wallace thought their son must have seen something like it on TV. Anyway, they repeated the ritual every year.

First the lights were turned out and they stood around a table with a big red candle, each holding a small white taper. Then Mike solemnly explained to Barbara, "Dad will light the red candle and then we'll all light our little candles from the big one."

When the five small wicks were flaming, he continued, "Now here is the special thing. When you mix your fire with my fire, it means we're friends forever. Watch!" He demonstrated by merging the flame of his candle with Susan's. "Now, Barbara, you do it with me," he directed, and slowly she brought her candle to his.

Last to meld the flames as the ritual continued around the circle were pupil and teacher. Helen saw that Barbara had managed to spot her new Christmas dress with hot wax—but she also saw that the child's eyes themselves were like candles in the semidarkness.

After the candle ceremony and Christmas Day, the rest of the holidays were anticlimax. Helen had planned to catch up on her reading, but spent the time altering clothes for Barbara and thinking up special things for her to do. Despite all their best efforts, Barbara seemed to be saying, "I can never be a part of you. Just let me watch."

Two days before vacation was over, the landlady called to say Barbara could come home because her father had returned. She did not say good-bye to the children or show any regret about leaving. She simply walked to the car with her greatly increased bundle of belongings and got in.

Was it worth it? Helen wondered, watching Wallace back the car down the drive. She remembered wryly the private moments she had wanted to share with Wallace when this strange little girl with observant eyes followed their every move, the times the four of them had interrupted their laughter over family jokes because they suddenly realized Barbara was left out. She was not even sure Barbara had wanted to come. Perhaps she had friends at the Children's Home. Perhaps she would have had a better time there. There was so much, Helen felt as she turned from the window, that she could never understand.

The first day back at school was typically Januaryish. Somehow Helen felt as dull and gray inside as the day itself, even though she had made a point of putting on the becoming red jersey she'd bought at one of the after Christmas clearance sales. Most of the children were wearing some new Christmas garment, and Barbara too appeared in her Christmas Day dress, with egg stains added now to the candle grease. Obviously the jeweled hairbrush had not been overused.

"It wasn't worth it," Helen whispered to herself. Nothing that had happened had any meaning to Barbara—nothing would carry over to make her life richer. She and Wallace and Mike and Susan had acted as baby-sitters and given the girl some warm clothing. That was the sum of it and she might as well write it off and forget it.

But the children were not ready to forget Christmas, and Helen allowed them half an hour's "telling time." To many in the class, the high point of Christmas had been decorating the tree, or the fun they'd had spending their own shopping money, or the new bike. Peter told about going to midnight mass for the first time. Esther told the class about her family's celebration of Hanukkah.

When Barbara's turn came, several moments elapsed in silence, and the girl seemed glued to her chair. Helen realized with a pang that Barbara had nothing to say. Nothing had happened that had any lasting meaning for her. As gently as possible she said, "You don't have to tell us anything, Barbara. It's up to you."

"But I do want to tell it," Barbara said. "It's just that I don't know what it's called—the thing with the candles."

"That doesn't matter," said Peter. "Tell us anyway."

Thus encouraged, Barbara slipped from her seat and moved to face the class. "Well, at our house last night we had Christmas. It's something you do with candles, but my dad and I didn't have any candles so we used matches instead. We each struck a match and then we held them close together so the fire mixed, and then—then we were friends for life."

She looked proudly about the roomful of children, awed by her mystical little tale, and suddenly she broke into a radiant smile. "It was the very nicest Christmas I ever had in my life." And finally, Helen understood.

*Home should be a retreat to which a son or daughter
can return in triumph or defeat,
in victory or disgrace,
and know they will be loved.*

Author unknown

Uncle Bun

Jan Nations

Uncle Bun was a charmer. He didn't visit very often, but his occasional visits to my childhood home during the 1940s and 1950s changed everything for whatever period of time he was there. I was one of eight children, and most of our excitement came from making mud pies, playing with June bugs and lightning bugs, and building a playhouse in the former chicken coop.

In our eyes, Uncle Bun was a world traveler. Whenever he came for a visit, he would tell us stories about where he'd been and the people he'd met. He brought all of us a new perspective on life. He usually had a wonderful present for each of us—and sometimes we would walk to the small country store in town where he would buy an entire brown bag of penny candy. That bag looked enormous when I was a little girl.

We never knew when we might hear from Uncle Bun. I attributed that to the fact that his "career"—whatever that was—kept him far too busy to plan ahead. Sometimes, instead of a visit, he'd send a huge box full of special surprises, things we'd never seen before. No children have ever been more delighted than we were as we unpacked those brown cardboard treasure chests of love.

I remember thinking how very rich Uncle Bun must have been to afford such fancy things. I couldn't help but compare this exciting and generous uncle with my own father—a simple man with a simple life working in the lead mines and taking on handyman jobs when he could in order to maintain a home for his wife and family. I loved my dad, and I knew he was a good man. But his life was unglamorous compared to his jovial brother with the twinkle in his eye, the wide grin, and the fascinating stories.

Uncle Bun always phoned us a day or two before his visit, and as soon as Dad would hang up the phone and tell us who called, the excitement would begin to build. We adored Uncle Bun and looked forward to this welcome break in our routine.

What I didn't know as a child was that, when Uncle Bun called, Dad drove into town and wired money to him from the small savings he'd put aside. Every penny Uncle Bun spent on us actually came from my father. Over the years, the pieces started falling into place: Uncle Bun's many travels were by train—riding unticketed in the back of freight cars. His stories were of people who rode with him, and they were all slightly embellished.

I'll never know why Uncle Bun chose to live the way he did, or why my dad kept his secret all those years. What I do know is that, in a situation where it would have been easy to take the credit himself, my dad carried on an unselfish act for years. Through Uncle Bun, Dad gave us gifts from places he'd never travel. And through us, Uncle Bun was part of a family and received the love he didn't see in the lonely life he lived. From my father, who never said a word, I learned what selfless, unconditional love is all about.

Gingham Aprons

Dorothy Canfield Fisher
from A Harvest of Stories

Many years ago when my great-grandmother was a frisky, withered old woman, she heard that on one of the mountain farms way up on a steep side road, the farmer's wife never came down to the village to buy things or go to church because she was afraid people would laugh at her. Her mother had been an Indian, and her skin was very dark. They were plain folks with little money, and she didn't think her clothes were good enough to go to church. She'd stayed away from people so long that she was shy—the way a deer is shy—and went into the house quickly and hid if a stranger happened to stop at the farm.

My great-grandmother no sooner heard that, than she got into the small, battered old family phaeton and had a boy drive her to the Hunter farm. Mrs. Hunter was hanging out her clothes on the lines when Great-grandmother drove into the yard. Before she could dodge away and hide, Great-grandmother hopped out of the low, little carriage and said, "Here, let me help you!" In a minute, with her mouth full of clothespins, she was standing by Mrs. Hunter, pinning up sheets and towels, and men's shirts. "My, how clean you get them!" she said mumblingly around the clothespins. "They're white as new milk! How do you make your soap? Do you put any salt in it?"

By the time they had the big basket of wet clothes hung up, the dark-skinned, black-haired mountain wife couldn't feel shy of the quick-stepping little old woman from the valley. They had a pleasant time talking in the kitchen as they washed the breakfast dishes, and sat down together to the basket of mending. The question of going to church came up, along with all sorts of other subjects. Before the old visitor had gone, Mrs. Hunter said she would go to church the next Sunday, if she could go with Great-grandmother and sit in the same pew with her.

Sure enough, the next Sunday, Great-grandmother, her young-lady daughter and her little-girl granddaughter stood on their front porch. They were all in their best Sunday dresses, wore bonnets, had their prayer books in their hands. They smiled at Mrs. Hunter as Mr. Hunter drove her up in the lumbering farm wagon.

Mrs. Hunter had a bonnet on over her sleek black hair. It was a cool day, she had put on a warm cloak, her shoes were brightly black with polish. And (she was a real country-woman whose idea of dressing up was a freshly ironed clean apron) she had put on a big blue-checked gingham apron, nicely starched, over her coat, and tied the string in the back.

My aunt, who was Great-grandmother's granddaughter, and who was the little girl on the front porch that day, said she and her young-lady aunt were so astonished to see a woman starting to church with a big apron on, over her coat, that their eyes opened wide, and they were just ready to put their hands up to their mouths to hide a smile. But Great-grandmother swung the little girl sharply around and shoved her back into the house, calling over her shoulder to Mrs. Hunter, "Well, would you believe it, the girls and I have forgotten to put our aprons on. We won't keep you waiting a minute."

Once inside, she hustled them into gingham aprons, which they tied on over their coats. She herself put on the biggest one she had, tied the strings in a dashing bow knot behind, and they sailed across to the church with Mrs. Hunter, aproned from chin to hem, all four of them.

People already in their pews looked astonished, but Great-grandmother put on a hard expression she sometimes used, and faced them down, so that they got the idea and made their children stop giggling.

At the end of the service, everybody came to shake hands with Mrs. Hunter. They knew Great-grandmother would have a thing or two to say to them, if they didn't. They told her and the rector of the church told her they were glad to see her out at church and they hoped she'd come often. After that Mrs. Hunter came every Sunday, the rest of her life—without an apron; for some time during the next week, Great-grandmother let fall negligently that it wasn't really necessary to wear them on Sundays.

*How far you go in life
depends on your being tender with the young,
compassionate with the aged,
sympathetic with the striving,
and tolerant of the weak and the strong—
because someday you will have been all of these.*

George Washington Carver

Rosa's Pretty Pink Shoes

Janet Lee Carey

When Mrs. Jeano passes out the papers, she walks by Rosa's desk. She doesn't leave a paper there, because Rosa's desk is empty. It has been empty for a long time.

Rosa and I used to run through the long grass all around the edges of the playground. I ran behind and watched her long black braid bounce in the wind like the tail of a horse.

Then, one day, Rosa didn't come to school. Mrs. Jeano put her hand on Rosa's empty desk. "There's been an accident," she said. "Rosa was hit by a car yesterday, and she is in the hospital. After school she chased her soccer ball into the street without stopping to look."

When I heard what had happened, my stomach felt cold—as if I had swallowed a handful of ice. At recess I took three sips from the drinking fountain. The water slid down my tongue, but it didn't melt the ice inside my stomach. I sat in the long grass where Rosa and I used to run.

Everyone in school was sad and afraid for Rosa. She stayed in the hospital for five weeks. The doctors fixed all the broken bones in her arm and in her legs. They said Rosa will walk again. But not for a long time.

Today Rosa comes back to school, but her chair will still be empty.

"Hey Christa!" she calls as she rolls into the classroom in her shiny wheelchair.

"Hey Rosa!" I yell back.

She is smiling. On her legs are two pink casts, and on her feet are new pink tennis shoes.

At recess I help push Rosa outside. It's hard to get her wheelchair through the door.

Rosa watches us jump rope. "No more homework. No more books!" she sings while I jump.

"Hey Rosa!" I shout. "Watch me on the bars!" But she doesn't watch. She looks at her shoes instead. I run over to her chair, braid her pink ribbon into her thick black hair, and whisper, "Don't worry, Rosa. You'll run again."

"I know," she says, "but my shoes..."

I know what she means. The pretty pink shoes don't look right on her feet. Rosa's shoes used to be brown with school-yard dirt.

"You want us to break them in for you?" I ask.

"Sure!"

"Hey Susie! Hey Scott! Come here."

We take off Rosa's new pink shoes. The girls take turns jumping rope in Rosa's shoes. Then we scrape them on the playground and play hopscotch in them. The boys shoot Rosa's shoes down the slide. They toss them around like footballs and stomp on them while Rosa laughs.

"Children!" yells Mrs. Jeano. "What are you doing with Rosa's shoes?"

"Breaking them in!" shouts Rosa. I help her put her shoes back on. The pink is streaked with brown. I tie each dirty lace into a bow. Now they look like Rosa's shoes. The bell rings, and I help wheel Rosa back inside. She snaps her fingers to the clicking sound the wheelchair makes. I skip as I push her wheelchair down the hall.

When Rosa runs again, she'll race with me through the tall grass, her long braid bouncing like the tail of a horse. I'm glad I helped her break in her new shoes. Now they're ready for the day when Rosa will run again.

A Brother's Lesson

Christopher de Vinck
from The Power of the Powerless

I grew up in the house where my brother was on his back in his bed for almost 33 years, in the same corner of his room, under the same window, beside the same yellow walls. Oliver was blind, mute. His legs were twisted. He didn't have the strength to lift his head nor the intelligence to learn anything.

Today I am an English teacher, and each time I introduce my class to the play about Helen Keller, "The Miracle Worker," I tell my students about Oliver. One day, during my first year teaching, a boy in the last row raised his hand and said, "Oh, Mr. de Vinck. You mean he was a vegetable."

I stammered for a few seconds. My family and I fed Oliver. We changed his diapers, hung his clothes and bed linen on the basement line in winter, and spread them out white and clean on the lawn in the summer. I always liked to watch the grasshoppers jump on the pillowcases.

We bathed Oliver. Tickled his chest to make him laugh. Sometimes we left the radio on in his room. We pulled the shade down over his bed in the morning to keep the sun from burning his tender skin. We listened to him laugh as we watched television downstairs. We listened to him rock his arms up and down to make the bed squeak. We listened to him cough in the middle of the night.

"Well, I guess you could call him a vegetable. I called him Oliver, my brother. You would have liked him."

One October day in 1946, when my mother was pregnant with Oliver, her second son, she was overcome by fumes from a leaking coal-burning stove. My oldest brother was sleeping in his crib, which was quite high off the ground so the gas didn't affect him. My father pulled them outside, where my mother revived quickly.

On April 20, 1947, Oliver was born. A healthy looking, plump, beautiful boy.

One afternoon, a few months later, my mother brought Oliver to a window. She held him there in the sun, the bright good sun, and there Oliver looked and looked directly into the sunlight, which was the first moment my mother realized that Oliver was blind. My parents, the true heroes of this story, learned, with the passing months, that blindness was only part of the problem. So they brought Oliver to Mt. Sinai Hospital in New York for tests to determine the extent of his condition.

The doctor said that he wanted to make it very clear to both my mother and father that there was absolutely nothing that could be done for Oliver. He didn't want my parents to grasp at false hope. "You could place him in an institution," he said. "But," my parents replied, "he is our son. We will take Oliver home of course." The good doctor answered, "Then take him home and love him."

Oliver grew to the size of a ten-year-old. He had a big chest, a large head. His hands and feet were those of a five-year-old, small and soft. We'd wrap a box of baby cereal for him at Christmas and place it under the tree; pat his head with a damp cloth in the middle of a July heat wave. His baptismal certificate hung on the wall above his head. A bishop came to the house and confirmed him.

Even now, five years after his death from pneumonia on March 12, 1980, Oliver still remains the weakest, most helpless human being I ever met, and yet he was one of the most powerful human beings I ever met. He could do absolutely nothing except breathe, sleep, eat, and yet he was responsible for action, love, courage, insight. When I was small my mother would say, "Isn't it wonderful that you can see?" And once she said, "When you go to heaven, Oliver will run to you, embrace you, and the first thing he will say is 'Thank you.'" I remember, too, my mother explaining to me that we were blessed with Oliver in ways that were not clear to her at first.

So often parents are faced with a child who is severely retarded, but who is also hyperactive, demanding or wild, who needs constant care. So many people have little choice but to place their child in an institution. We were fortunate that Oliver didn't need to be in his room all day. He never knew what his condition was. We were blessed with his presence, a true presence of peace.

When I was in my early 20s I met a girl and fell in love. After a few months I brought her home to meet my family. When my mother went to the kitchen to prepare dinner, I asked the girl, "Would you like to see Oliver?" for I had told her about my brother. "No," she answered.

Soon after, I met Roe, a lovely girl. She asked me the names of my brothers and sisters. She loved children. I thought she was wonderful. I brought her home after a few months to meet my family. Soon it was time for me to feed Oliver. I remember sheepishly asking Roe if she'd like to see him. "Sure," she said.

I sat at Oliver's bedside as Roe watched over my shoulder. I gave him his first spoonful, his second. "Can I do that?" Roe asked with ease, with freedom, with compassion, so I gave her the bowl and she fed Oliver one spoonful at a time.

The power of the powerless. Which girl would you marry? Today Roe and I have three children.

The Inspiration of Models

Rebecca Manley Pippert
from A Heart Like This

My very dear friends and neighbors, Jim and Ruth Nyquist, have been powerful role models of compassion to me and my children. For example, they once made a promise to Jim's relative Arloween, who was more like a sister than a cousin, that they would care for her in her old age if she ever became unable to care for herself. Because Arloween and her husband, Ev, were childless, they had poured their lives into a ministry to the young. Then several years after her husband's death, 81-year-old Arloween fell and suffered several minor strokes. They brought her to their home to recuperate, and decided that the time to fulfill their promise had come. She now lives with them permanently.

When my children first met Arloween, she was frail and struggling, though the beauty of her character still shone through. However, gradually over the weeks and months, the children began to see a different person emerge. Through the enormous love and encouragement of Ruth and Jim, Arloween began to gain strength and to participate in lively discussions at the table. Her comments always reflected great wisdom and insight, and she even began to make jokes. Every time we saw her she seemed more alive, with a deeper twinkle in her eye. Even her ability to cope with short-term memory loss astounded my children. When Elizabeth asked her if she had enjoyed helping us put up the art in our home the day before, Arloween answered, "I'm sorry, I don't remember being at your house yesterday. But I have two questions for you: Did I have a good time and did I do a good job?" Of course we all roared with laughter, but later Elizabeth said, "Oh, Mom, I hope I'm that cheerful if something like that ever happens to me." Many times after being in the Nyquist home, the children would say, "Boy, Arloween is getting so much better. That's because she's being loved so well."

Once when the Nyquists were away for a week, I suggested that we go over and set up the house for a "welcome home." I braced myself for comments like, "Mother, I have homework," or "Can't I have a friend over?" There have certainly been times in the past when I suggested doing things for people and heard initial grumbling and complaining! But not this time. They could hardly wait! They cut flowers from the Nyquists' marvelous English garden, and we arranged them in every room. The children sorted their mail, wrote them cards, and helped me set the table and prepare a meal. They worked feverishly and with joy to make the homecoming special.

After we finished our labors and went from room to room to inspect our work, David said, "Mom, doesn't it make you feel good to do something kind for people like the Nyquists who help...oh, you know, the world?" Later, I said to Elizabeth, "The Nyquists and Arloween are going to be so happy to see how pretty everything looks. They had to leave things a bit spartan since they would be gone for a while." Elizabeth looked at me with a horrified expression and said, "Mother! How could you ever say this house is spartan when it is so full of the love of God? You feel it the minute you walk in this door. Just look at what has happened to Arloween!"

I have never been so grateful to stand corrected in my life. In a low moment, Arloween once said, "Becky, I just wish the Lord would take me home to heaven. I don't know why I'm still here." And I answered her, "Well, I can give you two reasons why the Lord has kept you. You have no idea what your grace and courage in difficulty, and Jim and Ruth's love and compassion and generosity, have modeled to my children. If for no other reason than two little lives, I thank the Lord he has kept you."

Compassion is contagious. Let's catch it—and expose ourselves and our children to goodness every chance we get!

When God measures a man,
He puts the tape around the heart
instead of the head.

Author unknown

Sunday Best

Dorothy Canfield Fisher
from A Harvest of Stories

One of the families in our town was very poor. The father had died, the mother was sick, the five children scratched along as best they could, with what help the neighbors could give them. But they had to go without things that you'd think were necessary.

They wore things that other people had given up because they were too ragged. Their mother, sitting up in bed, patched them as best she could, and the children wore them. When the oldest boy—he was a little fellow about fourteen years old—got a chance to go to work for a farmer over the mountain from our valley, he had nothing at all to wear but a very old shirt, some faded, much-patched blue denim coveralls, and his work shoes.

The farmer and his wife had never seen anybody in such poor working clothes. It did not occur to them that the new-hired boy had no others at all. Saturday when the farmer's wife went to the village to sell some eggs, she bought young David a pair of blue jeans, so stiff they could almost stand alone—you know how brand-new overalls look.

The next day at breakfast they said they were going to church, and would David like to go along? Yes, indeed he would! So they went off to their rooms to get into their Sunday clothes. The farmer was dressed first, and sat down by the radio to get the time signals to set his watch. David walked in. His hair was combed slick with lots of water, his work shoes were blacked, his face was clean as a china plate. And he had on those stiff, new blue jeans, looking as though they were made out of blue stovepipe.

The farmer opened his mouth to say, "We're almost ready

to start. You'll be late if you don't get dressed for church,"
when he saw David's face. It was shining. He looked down at
the blue jeans with a smile; he ran his hand lovingly over their
stiff newness, and said ardently to the farmer, "Land! I'm so
much obliged to you folks for getting me these new clothes in
time to go to church in them."

The farmer had to blow his nose real hard before he could
say, "Wait a minute." He went to take off his own black suit
and put on a pair of blue jeans. Then he and David walked
into church together, sat in the same pew, and sang out of the
same hymnbook.

The Guest Book

Carla Muir

When I was young, I'd visit folks
who lived on neighboring streets.
A widow often asked me in
for tea and pastry treats.

She made me feel special with
a table set just so,
while she would talk of baking and
how long to raise the dough.

Politely, I would listen although
thoughts would often stray.
Each time I left, I gave my word
I'd come another day.

Before I went to college
she asked that I stop by.
She opened up her old guest book
while trying not to cry.

Then as she paged through many years,
in pen I saw my name.
For she had written in that book
the days and times I came.

"You won't learn this in textbooks,"
she softly said to me—
"how you can lift another's soul
with just a cup of tea."

"O-h-h-h Me"

Alan D. Wright
from A Chance at Childhood Again

N ot knowing what else to do, I stood motionless behind the grown son who held the hand of his dying father. It was my first church, my first month. I had never walked the road of cancer with a parishioner before. I was almost surprised at how deeply I cared for the man in the hospital bed. I didn't understand yet that God planned for me to love that bedridden man like Christ loved him. I didn't know yet that when God ordains a pastor, He provides the pastor's heart. So I just stood silently, surprised by the depth of my love, but disappointed by my feelings of pastoral ineptness.

Lester winced with pain. His medication at the time wasn't strong enough to mask his physical anguish. So his body constricted because of the pain emanating from his bones. He drew in a short breath and then exhaled slowly. As he breathed outward, Lester rhythmically stretched out a moan. "O-h-h-h me." It was a pain-filled, mournful moan. But, at the same time, it possessed a compelling beauty. It was not just a cry of distress. It was a sigh of the soul. The more I listened, the more it sounded like a song rather than a moan. "O-h-h-h me. O-h-h-h me."

The tender son leaned forward. I had been to seminary. I had been trained. But I watched this son carefully. His confident demeanor proved he knew how to care for his beloved father better than I. With a clasped hand and a hint of a smile, the son brought his face down close to his dad's.

Lester moaned again, "O-h-h-h me."

Then, what I could never imagine to happen occurred. The son echoed back, "O-h-h-h me."

The white-haired patient moaned louder, "O-h-h-h me."

Again, the unfathomable echo came back from the son, "O-h-h-h me."

What was I beholding? Was such insensitivity possible? Could a son actually mock his dying father's moan?

I considered interrupting the son's echo of anguish. I contemplated pulling the man away from the bed to save his father from the humiliation. But, oddly, Lester seemed comforted, not agitated by his son's peculiar imitation. So, I stood silently and waited.

I was about to learn a holy lesson in compassion that I would never forget.

After watching this amazing father-son duet of moans for some time, I stepped out of the hospital room with the son. He explained.

When I first met this saintly, aging man, he was at home, not in the hospital. Though Lester's health was declining rapidly and his pain was increasing at the same rate, there was no place of healing like home. Lester was thankful for a fine hospital, but the hospital had no home-cooked meals, no view of Rose of Sharon Road, and no Wesley.

Wesley was Lester's two-year-old grandson. I knew this toddler to be a blond-haired barrel of fun who was bound to bring sunshine to the darkest of days. I had seen Lester's smile broaden when Wesley was around. I know that Wesley's presence helped alleviate Lester's anguish. I knew how much he loved the little boy. But what Lester's son told me outside the hospital room that day touched my heart forever.

At home, as Lester's health worsened, he rarely walked. When he did, Lester supported himself with a walker. Each grueling step brought shooting pain. And with each step forward, each lift of the walker, Lester would exhale his usual moan. "O-h-h-h me." Step. "O-h-h-h me." Step.

One day, unprompted, little Wesley came alongside his shuffling, moaning grandfather. He placed his two-year-old hand at the base of Lester's walker, and with each painful step, Wesley "helped." With all his two-year-old strength, Wesley helped lift the walker upward and forward.

And following each of Lester's mournful moans, a two-year-old voice echoed back. "O-h-h me. O-h-h me."

Although I would like to have beheld the scene firsthand, I am more nourished by the picture I carry of it in my imagination. How different the man and the boy. There were more than seventy years between them. One had lived a lifetime; the other had hardly lived. One had bones brittle enough to make every trip down the hall risky, the other had bones supple enough to bounce on beds and fall off couches unharmed.

And yet, as Wesley echoed his grandfather's moan, how similar they were. Though the toddler was quicker, the size of their stride was about the same. Though Lester was a friendly talker, when in pain, his vocabulary was not much larger than little Wesley's. The old man and the little boy had a unique, beautiful connection as they walked around and moaned together.

My seminary professors and pastoral mentors had taught me consistently, but never so powerfully or eloquently as that two-year-old boy, the most important pastoral lesson of all. When people are hurting their worst, our words need to be fewest. Aching saints do not need long-winded preachers or glib cheerleaders. They need someone who will come alongside them and, step by grueling step, acknowledge their pain. Hurting people need someone who, in the apostle Paul's words, will "mourn with those who mourn."

The Flower

John R. Ramsey

For some time a person has provided me with a rose boutonniere to pin on the lapel of my suit every Sunday. Because I always got a flower on Sunday morning, I really did not think much of it. It was a nice gesture that I appreciated, but it became routine. One Sunday, however, what I considered ordinary became very special.

As I was leaving the Sunday service a young man approached me. He walked right up to me and said, "Sir, what are you going to do with your flower?" At first I did not know what he was talking about but then I understood.

I said, "Do you mean this?" as I pointed to the rose pinned to my coat.

He said, "Yes, sir. I would like it if you are just going to throw it away." At this point I smiled and gladly told him that he could have my flower, casually asking him what he was going to do with it. The little boy, who was probably less than ten years old, looked up at me and said, "Sir, I'm going to give it to my granny. My mother and father got divorced last year. I was living with my mother, but when she married again, she wanted me to live with my father. I lived with him for a while, but he said I could not stay, so he sent me to live with my grandmother. She is so good to me. She cooks for me and takes care of me. She has been so good to me that I want to give that pretty flower to her for loving me."

When the little boy finished I could hardly speak. My eyes filled with tears and I knew I had been touched in the depths of my soul. I reached up and unpinned my flower. With the flower in my hand, I looked at the boy and said, "Son, that is the nicest thing I have ever heard, but you can't have just this flower because it's not enough. If you'll look in front of the pulpit, you'll see a big bouquet of flowers. Please take those flowers to your granny because she deserves the very best."

If I hadn't been touched enough already, he made one last statement and I will always cherish it. He said, "What a wonderful day! I asked for one flower but got a beautiful bouquet."

It is when we forget ourselves
that we do things that will be remembered.

Author unknown

Encouragement

FROM THE MOUND

When I'd finally connect with the ball—oh, man, I knew I deserved the hit. I'd be going all the way down the first-base line. I'd turn to look at my father on the pitcher's mound. He'd take off his glove and tuck it under his arm, and then clap for me. To my ears, it sounded like a standing ovation at Yankee Stadium.

Beth Mullally
from A Lesson from the Mound,
quoted from Reader's Digest

Teardrops of Hope

Nancy Sullivan Geng
Reprinted with permission from
The September 1991 Reader's Digest

My friend Lauri and I had brought out our kids to the park that day to celebrate my 35th birthday. From a picnic table we watched them laugh and leap through the playground while we unpacked a basket bulging with sandwiches and cookies.

We toasted our friendship with bottles of mineral water. It was then that I noticed Lauri's new drop earrings. In the thirteen years I'd known Lauri, she'd always loved drop earrings. I'd seen her wear pair after pair: threaded crystals cast in blue, strands of colored gemstones, beaded pearls in pastel pink.

"There's a reason why I like drop earrings," Lauri told me.

She began revealing images of a childhood that changed her forever, a tale of truth and its power to transform.

It was a spring day. Lauri was in sixth grade, and her classroom was cheerfully decorated. Yellow May Day baskets hung suspended on clotheslines above desks, caged hamsters rustled in shredded newspaper and orange marigolds curled over cutoff milk cartons on window shelves.

The teacher, Mrs. Lake, stood in front of the class, her auburn hair flipping onto her shoulders like Jackie Kennedy's, her kind, blue eyes sparkling. But it was her drop earrings that Lauri noticed most—golden teardrop strands laced with ivory pearls. "Even from my back-row seat," Lauri recalled, "I could see those earrings gleaming in the sunlight from the windows."

Mrs. Lake reminded the class it was the day set aside for end-of-the-year conferences. Both parents and students would participate in these important progress reports. On the black-board, an alphabetical schedule assigned twenty minutes for each family.

Lauri's name was at the end of the list. But it didn't matter much. Despite at least one reminder letter mailed home and the phone calls her teacher had made, Lauri knew her parents would not be coming.

Lauri's father was an alcoholic, and that year his drinking had escalated. Many nights Lauri would fall asleep hearing the loud, slurred voice of her father, her mother's sobs, slamming doors, pictures rattling on the wall.

The previous Christmas Lauri and her sister had saved baby-sitting money to buy their dad a shoeshine kit. They had wrapped the gift with red-and-green paper and trimmed it with a gold ribbon curled into a bow. When they gave it to him on Christmas Eve, Lauri watched in stunned silence as he threw it across the living room, breaking it into three pieces.

Now Lauri watched all day long as each child was escorted to the door leading into the hallway, where parents would greet their sons or daughters with proud smiles, pats on the back and sometimes even hugs. The door would close, and Lauri would try to distract herself with her assignments. But she couldn't help hearing the muffled voices as parents asked questions, children giggled nervously and Mrs. Lake spoke. Lauri imagined how it might feel to have her parents greet her at the door.

When at last everyone else's name had been called, Mrs. Lake opened the door and motioned for Lauri. Silently Lauri slipped out into the hallway and sat down on a folding chair. Across from the chair was a desk covered with student files and projects. Curiously she watched as Mrs. Lake looked through the files and smiled.

Embarrassed that her parents had not come, Lauri folded her hands and looked down at the linoleum. Moving her desk chair next to the downcast little girl, Mrs. Lake lifted Lauri's chin so she could make eye contact. "First of all," the teacher began, "I want you to know how much I love you."

Lauri lifted her eyes. In Mrs. Lake's face she saw things she'd rarely seen: compassion, empathy, tenderness.

"Second," the teacher continued, "you need to know it is not your fault that your parents are not here today."

Again Lauri looked into Mrs. Lake's face. No one had ever talked to her like this. No one.

"Third," she went on, "you deserve a conference whether or not your parents are here or not. You deserve to hear how well you are doing and how wonderful I think you are."

In the following minutes, Mrs. Lake held a conference just for Lauri. She showed Lauri her grades. She scanned Lauri's papers and projects, praising her efforts and affirming her strengths. She had even saved a stack of watercolors Lauri had painted.

Lauri didn't know exactly when, but at some point in that conference she heard the voice of hope in her heart. And somewhere a transformation started.

As tears welled in Lauri's eyes, Mrs. Lake's face became misty and hazy—except for her drop earrings of golden curls and ivory pearls. What were once irritating intruders in oyster shells had been transformed into things of beauty.

It was then that Lauri realized, for the first time in her life, that she was lovable.

As we sat together in a comfortable silence, I thought of all the times Lauri had worn the drop earrings of truth for me.

I, too, had grown up with an alcoholic father, and for years I had buried my childhood stories. But Lauri had met me in a symbolic hallway of empathy. There she helped me see that the shimmering jewel of self-worth is a gift from God that everyone deserves. She showed me that even adulthood is not too late to don the dazzling diamonds of new-found self-esteem.

Just then the kids ran up and flopped onto the grass to dramatize their hunger. For the rest of the afternoon we wiped spilled milk, praised off-balance somersaults and glided down slides much too small for us.

But in the midst of it all, Lauri handed me a small box, a birthday gift wrapped in red floral paper trimmed with a gold bow.

I opened it. Inside was a pair of drop earrings.

Affirming words from moms and dads are like light switches. Speak a word of affirmation at the right moment in a child's life and it's like lighting up a whole roomful of possibilities.

Gary Smalley
from Leaving the Light On

Mother Earned Her Wrinkles

Erma Bombeck
from Forever Erma

According to her height and weight on the insurance charts, she should be a guard for the Lakers.

She has iron-starved blood, one shoulder is lower than the other, and she bites her fingernails.

She is the most beautiful woman I have ever seen. She should be. She's worked on that body and face for more than sixty years. The process for that kind of beauty can't be rushed.

The wrinkles on her face have been earned...one at a time. The stubborn one around the lips that deepened with every "No!" The thin ones on the forehead that mysteriously appeared when the first child was born.

The eyes are protected by glass now, but you can still see the perma-crinkles around them. Young eyes are darting and fleeting. These are mature eyes that reflect a lifetime. Eyes that have glistened with pride, filled with tears of sorrow, snapped in anger and burned from loss of sleep. They are now direct and penetrating and look at you when you speak.

The bulges are classics. They developed slowly from babies too sleepy to walk who had to be carried home from Grandma's, grocery bags lugged from the car, ashes carried out of the basement while her husband was at war. Now they are fed by a minimum of activity, a full refrigerator and TV bends.

The extra chin is custom-grown and takes years to perfect. Sometimes you can only see it from the side, but it's there. Pampered women don't have an extra chin. They cream them away or pat the muscles until they become firm. But this chin has always been there, supporting a nodding head that has slept in a chair all night...bent over knitting...praying.

The legs are still shapely, but the step is slower. They ran too often for the bus, stood a little too long when she clerked in a department store, got beat up while teaching her daughter how to ride a two wheeler. They're purple at the back of the knees.

The hands? They're small and veined and have been dunked, dipped, shook, patted, wrung, caught in doors, splintered, dyed, bitten and blistered, but you can't help but be impressed when you see the ring finger that has shrunk from years of wearing the same wedding ring. It takes time—and much more—to diminish a finger.

I looked at Mother long and hard the other day and said, "Mom, I have never seen you look so beautiful."

"I work at it," she snapped.

Some people, no matter how old they get,
never lose their beauty—
they merely move it from their faces into their hearts.

Author unknown

Look, Daddy, I Can Fly!

Becky Freeman
from Still Lickin' the Spoon

Although I love the slinky, silky gowns my husband gives me every holiday season, this year I asked if he might give me something a little less breezy. I was particularly interested in sleepwear that would wrap warm and snugly around my cold, cold feet.

Thinking it would be a cute joke, Scott gave me a pair of "woman size" pink and white feety pajamas—in a teddy bear print. Christmas evening, I stole away to the bedroom and tried them on just for fun. As I put one foot and then another into the pajama legs, I drifted back to the very first memory I have as a child. I could almost hear my daddy—as he sounded nearly thirty-five years ago—softly singing, "Put your little foot, put your little foot, put your little foot right here..." as I stood on my bed while he helped me into my feety pj's.

My father is one man who has managed, all his life, to keep his child-heart pumping strong.

One rainy spring afternoon, when I was about eleven, I went out to the garage to find my father ascending a ladder into the attic. Though Daddy was sentimental, he was *not* a handyman, so the sight of the ladder provoked my curiosity. Then he crooked his finger in a silent gesture that I knew meant, "Come along, but be quiet."

I followed him up into the attic and sat down beside him, curious as to the nature of our exploration. But all my dad said was, "Shhh...listen." Then I heard it. The rain, pattering overhead—amplified by our nearness to the rooftop.

"I come up here whenever it rains," Daddy said softly. It

was cool and comforting, a tender moment caught—like a snapshot—in my mind.

To my pleasant surprise, my husband turned out to be a rain-on-the-roof kind of guy, too. He even built our bed so that the head of it fits snug against a large picture window. At night, if the full moon is shining or a soft rain is falling, Scott pulls up the blinds and raises the window and whispers, "Shhh...Becky. Listen." And this, I believe, is part of the reason why the two men I love most in the whole world are my daddy and my husband.

Another amazing thing about Daddy: In all my years, I cannot ever recall my father criticizing me. Not once. Always, he would praise and encourage my efforts—however crazy, however childish.

Not long ago I had a dream; it is a reoccurring dream I've had for years. In it I can fly. I love these dreams, and while I'm in them, I cannot understand why other people don't just float themselves up to the sky and join me. It is so easy, nothing to it at all. Most of the time I just spread out my arms and take off, but in one of my dreams I piloted a Frisbee. Now *that* was fun!

But the last dream I had was especially realistic. Once again I was flying, and in my dream I thought to myself, *This is ridiculous. Nobody else is flying except me. I need to find out if this is real or if this is just my imagination.*

So I flew to my parents' home, knocked on the door, and floated up to the ceiling. Then I hovered over my father, who was looking up at me, not at all surprised to find me up there, and I said, "Daddy, listen. You've *got* to tell me the truth. I really think I'm flying. It feels so real. But I'm worried that this might just all be a dream."

My daddy's answer was swift and sure. "Honey," he said, "it's no dream. You're flying all right."

When I woke up I laughed, but then tears welled in my eyes. *How marvelous,* I thought, *that even in my subconscious, in spite of all logic to the contrary, I have a father who believes I can fly.*

For Father's Day last year, I could not find a card that seemed to fit how I felt about Daddy. However, I came across a scene in a children's book that turned out to be perfect. It was a scene with Piglet and Winnie-the-Pooh, walking side by side toward a setting sun. Their short conversation summed up exactly how I felt about my father through the years.

Piglet sidled up to Pooh from behind.

"Pooh!" he whispered.

"Yes, Piglet?"

"Nothing," said Piglet, taking Pooh's paw. "I just wanted to be sure of you."

My dad has been like Pooh to me, his Little Girl-Piglet. Oh, we don't chit-chat a whole lot, not like my mother and I anyway. But in every memory involving my father—from the time he sang, "Put your little foot" as he helped me into my feety pajamas, until this latest dream where he assured me that, yes, I could really fly—my father has been there in the shadows, cheering me on. He has given me the steadfast assurance that always, and forever, I can be sure of him.

Chance Meeting

Jane Kirkpatrick
from A Burden Shared

They shared a neighborhood and street, these friends, shared good memories, good times. When each wife became a widow within weeks of the other, they shared in mourning, too. The women made a pact that no hour would be too late to wake the other when the memories and loss became so great that only a friend's embrace could get them through. No need to call ahead, just knock on the other's door. Each agreed to give in this special way.

One night the grief became so great it woke her, the anguish so real it sliced through her troubled sleep. In her night dress, she fled into the darkness seeking solace at her neighbor's door. She did not make it. Instead, she met her friend mid-street, equally seeking, reaching for the comfort found only inside understanding arms.

Grandma's Garden

Lynnette Curtis

Each year, my Grandmother Inez planted tulips in her flower garden and looked forward to their springtime beauty with childlike anticipation. Under her loving guardianship, they sprang up each April faithfully, and she was never disappointed. But she said the real flowers that decorated her life were her grandchildren.

I, for one, was not going to play along.

I was sent to stay with my grandmother when I was sixteen years old. My parents lived overseas and I was a very troubled young woman, full of false wisdom and anger at them for their inability to cope with or understand me. An unhappy, disrespectful teenager, I was ready to drop out of school.

Grandma was a tiny woman, towered over by her own children and their not-yet-grown offspring, and she possessed a classic, old-fashioned prettiness. Her hair was dark and elegantly styled, and her eyes were of the clearest blue, vibrant, and glittering with energy and intensity. She was ruled by an extraordinary loyalty to family, and she loved as profoundly and sincerely as a child. Still, I thought my grandmother would be easier to ignore than my parents.

I moved into her humble farmhouse silently, skulking about with my head hung low and eyes downcast like an abused pet. I had given up on others, instead cocooning myself within a hard shell of apathy. I refused to allow another soul admittance to my private world because my greatest fear was that someone would discover my secret vulnerabilities. I was convinced life was a bitter struggle better fought on one's own.

I expected nothing from grandmother but to be left alone, and planned to accept nothing less. She, however, did not give up so easily.

School began and I attended classes occasionally, spending the rest of my days in my pajamas, staring dully at the television set in my bedroom. Not taking the hint, Grandma burst through my door each morning like an unwelcome ray of sunshine.

"Good morning!" she'd sing, cheerfully raising the blinds from my window. I pulled my blanket over my head and ignored her.

When I did stray from my bedroom, I was barraged with a string of well-meant questions from her regarding my health, my thoughts and my views on the world in general. I answered in mumbled monosyllables, but somehow she was not discouraged. In fact, she acted as if my meaningless grunts fascinated her; she listened with as much solemnity and interest as if we were engaged in an intense conversation in which I had just revealed an intimate secret. On those rare occasions when I happened to offer more than a one-word response, she would clap her hands together joyously and smile hugely, as if I had presented her with a great gift.

At first, I wondered if she just didn't get it. However, though she wasn't an educated woman, I sensed she had the simple common-sense smarts that come from natural intelligence. Married at age thirteen during the Great Depression, she learned what she needed to know about life by raising five children through difficult economic times, cooking in other people's restaurants and eventually running a restaurant of her own.

So I shouldn't have been surprised when she insisted I learn to make bread. I was such a failure at kneading that Grandma would take over at that stage of the process. However, she wouldn't allow me to leave the kitchen until the bread was set out to rise. It was during those times, when her attention was focused away from me and I stared at the flower garden outside the window of the kitchen, that I first began to talk to her. She listened with such eagerness that I was some-times embarrassed.

Slowly, as I realized my grandmother's interest in me did not wear off with the novelty of my presence, I opened up to her more and more. I began to secretly yet fervently look forward to our talks.

When the words finally came to me, they would not stop. I began attending school regularly, and rushed home each after-noon to find her sitting in her usual chair, smiling and waiting to hear a detailed account of the minutes of my day.

One day in my junior year, I hurried through the door to Grandma's side and announced, "I was named editor of the high school newspaper!"

She gasped and clapped her hands over her mouth. More moved than I could ever be, she seized both my hands in hers and squeezed them, fiercely. I looked into her eyes, which were sparkling like mad. She said, "I like you so much, and I am very proud of you!"

Her words hit me with such force that I couldn't respond. Those words did more for me than a thousand "I love you's." I knew her love was unconditional, but her friendship and pride were things to earn. To receive them both from this incredible woman made me begin to wonder whether there was, in fact, something likable and worthy within myself. She awakened in me a desire to discover my own potential, and a reason to allow others to know my vulnerabilities.

On that day, I decided to try to live as she did—with energy and intensity. I was suddenly flushed with an appetite to explore the world, my mind and the hearts of others, to love as freely and unconditionally as she had. And I realized that I loved her—not because she was my grandmother, but because she was a beautiful individual who had taught me what she knew about caring for herself and others.

My grandmother passed away in the springtime, nearly two

years after I came to live with her, and two months before I graduated from high school.

She died encircled by her children and grandchildren, who held hands and remembered a life filled with love and happiness. Before she left this world, each of us leaned over her bed, with moist eyes and faces, and kissed her tenderly. As my turn came, I kissed her gently on the cheek, took her hand and whispered, "I like you so much, Grandma, and I am very proud of you!"

Now, as I prepare to graduate from college, I often think of my grandmother's words, and hope she would still feel proud of me. I marvel at the kindness and patience with which she helped me emerge from a difficult childhood to a young womanhood filled with peace. I picture her in the springtime, as the tulips in her garden, and we, her offspring, still bloom with an enthusiasm equaled only by her own. And I continue to work to make sure she will never be disappointed.

Beauty Contest

Allison Harms

I won a beauty contest when I was in third grade. I didn't expect to. At nine years old, I already knew that my face was too full, that my eyes were set too closely together, that the angles of my chin and nose were too sharp. Besides, I wore glasses and my teeth were crooked. My body could not be called a "figure" except in geometric terms: I was a flat rectangle with a building block build. In addition to all my physical drawbacks, my older sister had informed me that I had the personality of overcooked cauliflower.

On the day of the contest, all these negative appraisals compounded my fears as I stood to be judged against a whole civilization of more beautiful girls. They had all arrived at school giggling in new dresses, shiny black patent leather shoes, curls, ribbons, even lipstick. I'm sure my dress was fine too and that my mother had done her best with my belligerently straight hair. I'd worn those pink sponge rollers overnight so at least my hair was doing something under my droopy ribbon. Still, I felt like I was facing a firing squad as the other classes filed in to watch the spectacle, laughing and pointing. When the teacher began to list the names of the contestants, I concentrated on trying to make time fast-forward so that I could avoid this moment. I imagined being home curled up in my reading chair with my book and my cat. Drinking cocoa and eating warm cinnamon toast. Another part of my mind was already comforting my soon-to-be-rejected self. "This doesn't matter," I told myself. "The judges aren't fair. They're just going to pick the teacher's pet."

A sudden hush interrupted all the pictures and voices in my head. Then my teacher's voice, my name, and loud cheers and clapping from the crowd. A small, rough ceramic disc was placed in my hand. As I translated the words scratched into its surface, that hard, red clay became a treasure in my hand. I read: "Allison—Most Brilliant." When I raised my eyes, I saw that all the other girls held a disc too. Still giggling nervously, they began passing around their awards. Through relief-filled eyes, I read some of their happiness: each disc was inscribed with a unique message of self-worth which had been designed even before the contest had begun. There had never really been a contest! And that was the whole point.

It must have been some creative teacher's idea: to counteract that destructive third grade project of comparing ourselves to each other, to demonstrate in three dimensions that each person has beauty, gifts, abilities. That there is beauty deeper than the surface *and* beauty in our differences, not in the fact that we fit into some uniform standard. I don't pretend that I learned that lesson once for all that day, but it was an ordeal-turned-episode to build on. And today, when I rediscovered a small ceramic disc under some papers at the back of a drawer, I felt my face shine with the happy surprise of finding myself valued. I silently thanked the teacher whose name I have forgotten. And I smiled at the memory of an awkward nine-year-old girl who looked into the mirror that teacher held up for her and saw herself as beautiful.

Sparky

Earl Nightingale
from More of... The Best of Bits and Pieces

For Sparky, school was all but impossible. He failed every subject in the eighth grade. He flunked physics in high school, getting a grade of zero.

Sparky also flunked Latin, algebra, and English. He didn't do much better in sports. Although he did manage to make the school's golf team, he promptly lost the only important match of the season. There was a consolation match; he lost that, too.

Throughout his youth, Sparky was awkward socially. He was not actually disliked by the other students; no one cared that much. He was astonished if a classmate ever said hello to him outside of school hours.

There's no way to tell how he might have done at dating. Sparky never once asked a girl to go out in high school. He was too afraid of being turned down.

Sparky was a loser. He, his classmates...everyone knew it. So he rolled with it. Sparky had made up his mind early in life that if things were meant to work out, they would. Otherwise he would content himself with what appeared to be his inevitable mediocrity.

However, one thing was important to Sparky—drawing. He was proud of his artwork. Of course, no one else appreciated it. In his senior year of high school, he submitted some cartoons to the editors of the yearbook. The cartoons were turned down. Despite this particular rejection, Sparky was so convinced of his ability that he decided to become a professional artist.

After completing high school, he wrote a letter to Walt Disney Studios. He was told to send some samples of his artwork, and the subject for a cartoon was suggested. Sparky drew the proposed cartoon. He spent a great deal of time on it and on all the other drawings he submitted. Finally, the reply came from Disney Studios. He had been rejected once again. *Another loss for the loser.*

So Sparky decided to write his own autobiography in cartoons. He described his childhood self—a little boy loser and chronic underachiever. The cartoon character would soon become famous worldwide.

For Sparky, the boy who had such a lack of success in school and whose work was rejected again and again, was Charles Schulz. He created the "Peanuts" comic strip and the little cartoon character whose kite would never fly and who never succeeded in kicking a football—Charlie Brown.

Perceptive?

Gary Smalley
from Home Remedies

S ixth grade hadn't been a banner year for Eric. Never very confident in school, he had a particular dread of mathematics. "A mental block," one of the school's counselors had told him. Then, as if a mental math block wasn't enough for an eleven-year-old kid to deal with, he came down with measles in the fall and had to stay out of school for two weeks. By the time he got back, his classmates were *multiplying* fractions. Eric was still trying to figure out what you got when you put a half pie with three-quarters of a pie...besides a lot of pie.

Eric's teacher, Mrs. Gunther—loud, overweight, terrifying, and a year away from retirement—was unsympathetic. For the rest of the year she called him "Measly" in honor of his untimely spots and hounded him with ceaseless makeup assignments. When his mental block prevented his progress in fractions, she would thunder at him in front of the class, "I don't give a Continental for your excuses! You'd better straighten up, Measly, them ain't wings I hear flappin'!"

The mental block, once the size of a backyard fence, now loomed like the Great Wall of China. Eric despaired of ever catching up, and even fell behind in subjects he'd been good at.

Then came a remarkable moment.

It happened in the middle of Mrs. Warwick's ninth grade English class. To this day, some twenty-five years later, Eric still lights up as he recalls the Moment.

The fifth period class had been yawning through Mrs. Warwick's attempts to spark discussion about a Mark Twain story. At some point in the lecture, something clicked in Eric's mind. It was probably crazy, but it suddenly seemed like he understood something Twain had been driving at—something a little below the surface. Despite himself, Eric raised his hand and ventured an observation.

That led to the moment when Mrs. Warwick looked straight into Eric's eyes, beamed with pleasure, and said, "Why, Eric...that was *very* perceptive of you!"

Perceptive. Perceptive? Perceptive!

The word echoed in Eric's thoughts for the rest of the day—and then for the rest of his life. *Perceptive? Me? Well, yeah. I guess that WAS perceptive. Maybe I AM perceptive.*

One word, one little positive word dropped at the right moment somehow tipped the balance in a teenager's view of himself—and possibly changed the course of his life. (Even though he still can't multiply fractions.)

Eric went on to pursue a career in journalism and eventually became a book editor, working successfully with some of the top authors in America.

Many teachers are well aware how praise motivates children. One teacher said she praised each student in her third grade class every day, without exception. Her students were the most motivated, encouraged, and enthusiastic in the school. I remember what happened when my high school geometry teacher began to affirm me regularly. Within six weeks my D average climbed to an A.

It's wonderful when a teacher has the opportunity to inject a word of affirmation into a child's life. But after years of counseling, we have concluded that the most powerful form of affirmation takes place *close to home....*

Twice Blessed

Kathryn Lay

On the day my husband and I learned of our imminent adoption of our nine-month-old daughter, we joyously took our closest friends out to dinner in celebration.

While we laughed and talked at the restaurant, telling them of what we knew about our soon-to-arrive and much-prayed-for daughter, I became aware that the older couple in the booth behind us laughed as we did and nodded knowingly as we voiced our excitement and nervousness.

After ten years of infertility, of prayers, and eight months of parenting classes and paperwork and home studies—we were full of joy at the good news. It bubbled over as we talked and planned in the restaurant.

When the couple behind us left their booth, they paused at our table.

"Congratulations," the woman said, patting my shoulder.

"Thank you," I said, grateful that they weren't angry at our loudness.

She leaned closer and said, "I have several children of my own. I have a granddaughter who was adopted by someone not long ago. I've never seen her. Hearing your excitement, I feel in my heart that somewhere she is loved and well taken care of by a family like you."

Patting my shoulder once more, she whispered, "I'll pray for you and your baby."

At a time when we were blessed and overflowing with joy, God put us in a place where we could be a blessing and comfort to another. I pray for that grandmother, that God will continue to give her peace and comfort for the granddaughter she wonders about. And I know that my husband and I were in her prayers that night.

I knew I was special to him—
that he was pulling for me
and praying for me
during each of the small crises that came my way.
It's what every little girl needs from a father.

Danae Dobson
from What My Parents Did Right

Art 101

Author unknown

When I was 34 years old and the mother of three children, I took Art 101 at Motlow State Community College in Tennessee. One day our instructor announced that the project we had done on the first day of class was to be included in the notebook that would be a major part of our grade. "May I do another project?" I asked somewhat anxiously. "I just don't have the first one anymore."

The instructor asked what had happened to it. Somewhat embarrassed, I replied, "It's on my mother's fridge."

A Gift from My Dad

Steve Dwinnells

I have a special box. It's a little, wooden box with two small, shiny handles and a tiny padlock. It's simple—no fancy engravings, no high-gloss finish, no felt-covered bottom. The edges don't fit together well, the hinges on the lid have begun to squeak.

But it's my box, and every now and again I take the small key and unlock the padlock. As I raise the lid, the box releases its special memories, and the memories take me back to another time and another place.

Inside the box are a few knickknacks and a letter. Not much value in the world's eyes, maybe, but a priceless treasure to me. This box was a gift from my dad.

One Christmas Dad made boxes for all three of us boys. He wasn't much of a carpenter. Some of the pieces aren't cut exactly right, and the joints don't fit together well.

But to me, a master carpenter couldn't have made anything better. The box's perfection isn't in its form, but in the motivation behind the making of it.

The box was made by big, callused hands that knew hard work; by a mind that understood what responsibility means; by a warm heart that loved me. Inside this box is a handwritten letter addressed to me by my dad. The letter will never be published or nominated for a literary award. It is just a simple letter expressing a tenderness that Dad didn't know how to say very well verbally. It is a note telling me how proud he was of me and that he loved me. In the only way that he knew, he told me that he was glad I was his son.

Dad died a few days after Christmas that year. He didn't leave much money or a big home. But he did leave me that box.

With a simple box and a simple message, he left me his love.

As the years have come and gone, the box has taken on even greater value to me as I have come to realize what it really symbolizes. It is a reminder that only the gifts of our hearts hold enduring value.

The smoothly sanded, varnished sides represent the hard work and the perseverance that I ought to strive for. The strength of the wood epitomizes the lasting strength that I need as I struggle through life's difficulties. The blemishes and the flaws reveal to me that perfection lies not in outward appearances. And like the letter inside, the box shows that warmth and love come from within, from the heart.

Like the box, I have nicks and rough edges, and my joints don't match up well. But just as a letter of fatherly love fills that box, I know that the perfect love of God fills me, making me a masterpiece.

Use what talents you possess—
the woods would be very silent
if no birds sang there except those that sang best.

Henry Van Dyke

Mistaken Identity

James Dobson
from Home with a Heart

Jaime Escalante, the Garfield High School teacher on whom the movie *Stand and Deliver* was based, once told me this story about a fellow teacher. During his first year in the classroom, he had two students name Johnny. One was a happy child, an excellent student, a fine citizen. The other Johnny spent much of his time goofing off and making a nuisance of himself.

When the PTA held its first meeting of the year, a mother came up to this teacher and said, "How's my son, Johnny, getting along?" He assumed she was the mom of the better student and replied, "I can't tell you how much I enjoy him. I'm so glad he's in my class."

The next day the problem child came to the teacher and said, "My mom told me what you said about me last night. I haven't ever had a teacher who wanted me in his class."

That day he completed his assignments and brought in his completed homework the next morning. A few weeks later, the "problem" Johnny had become one of this teacher's hardest working students—and one of his best friends. This misbehaving child's life was turned around all because he was mistakenly identified as a good student.

Not every lazy or underachieving boy or girl could be motivated by a simple compliment from a teacher, of course, but there is a principle here that applies to all kids: It's better to make a child stretch to reach your high opinion than stoop to match your disrespect.

Special Children, Mine and God's

Nancy Sullivan Geng

On a hot July morning, I awoke to the clicks of a broken fan blowing humid air across my face. That got me thinking about all the other things that had "broken down" in my life.

Parenting a daughter who has Down syndrome presents unique challenges. Although Sarah's heart surgery and many serious infections were over, now we faced catastrophic hospital bills. On top of that, my husband's job would be eliminated in just weeks, and losing our home seemed inevitable.

As I closed my eyes to try to put together a morning prayer, I felt a small hand nudge my arm. "Mommy," Sarah said, "I-I-I g-g-g-got r-r-ready for va-va-va-vacation Bi-Bi-Bible school all by myself!"

Next to the bed stood five-year-old Sarah, her eyes twinkling through thick, pink-framed glasses. Beaming with pride, she turned both palms up and exclaimed, "Ta-dah!"

I noticed her red-checked, seersucker shorts were on backward, with the drawstring stuck in the side waistband. A J.C. Penney price tag hung from the front of a new, green polka-dot top, also on backward. She had chosen unmatched red and green winter socks to go with the outfit. Her tennis shoes were on the wrong feet, and she wore a baseball cap with the visor and emblem turned backward.

"I-I-I packed a b-b-backpack, t-t-too!" she stuttered, while unzipping her bag so I could see what was inside. Curious, I peered in at the treasures she had so carefully packed: five Lego blocks, a box of unopened paper clips, a fork, an undressed

Cabbage Patch doll, three jigsaw puzzle pieces, and a crib sheet from the linen closet.

Gently lifting her chin until our eyes met, I said very slowly, "You look beautiful!"

"Thank y-y-you," Sarah smiled, as she began to twirl around like a ballerina.

Just then, the living room clock chimed 8:00, which meant I had 45 minutes to get myself, two toddlers, and a baby out the door.

As the morning minutes dissolved into urgent seconds, I realized I was not going to have time to change Sarah's outfit.

Buckling each child into a car seat, I tried to reason with Sarah. "Honey, I don't think you'll be needing your backpack for vacation Bible school. Why don't you let me keep it in the car for you?"

"No-o-o-o-o. I n-n-need it!"

And so I surrendered, telling myself her self-esteem was more important than what people might think of her knapsack full of useless stuff.

When we got to church, I attempted to redo Sarah's outfit with one hand while I held my baby in the other. But Sarah pulled away, reminding me of my early morning words, "No-o-o-o-o...I l-l-look b-b-beautiful!"

Overhearing our conversation, a young teacher joined us. "You *do* look beautiful!" the woman told Sarah. Then she took Sarah's hand and said to me, "You can pick up Sarah at 11:30. We'll take good care of her." As I watched them walk away, I knew Sarah was in good hands.

While Sarah was in school, I took the other two children and ran errands. All the while my thoughts raced with anxiety and disjointed prayer. What did the future hold? How would we provide for our three small children? Would we lose our home? These painful questions caused me to wonder if God loved us.

I got back to the church a few minutes early. A door to the sun-filled chapel had been propped open, and I could see the children seated inside in a semicircle listening to a Bible story.

Sarah, sitting with her back to me, was still clutching the canvas straps which secured her backpack. Her baseball cap, shorts, and shirt were still on backward.

Watching her from a distance, I became aware of warm emotion welling within. One thought rushed through my mind, one simple phrase: "I sure do love her."

Then, as I stood there, I heard that still, comforting voice that I have come to understand is God's—"That's the way I feel about *you*."

I closed my eyes and imagined my Creator looking at me from a distance: my life so much like Sarah's outfit—backward, unmatched, mixed up...

"Why are you holding that useless 'backpack' full of anxiety, doubt, and fear?" I could imagine God saying to me, "Let Me carry it."

I sensed that God was speaking not only to me, but to all those who struggle with lives that seem backward, inside-out, and out of control. We all want to be financially secure, free from illness, and immune to the inevitable pain that life brings. But God calls us to trust that what we need will be provided.

It is in these vulnerable times of weakness that we need to give our fear-filled backpack to the One who says, "You are precious in my eyes and I love you" (Isaiah 43:4).

That night as I once more turned on our crippled fan, I thanked God for the privilege of parenting Sarah. Through her, I realized, God had been revealed to me in a new way.

Virtue

HOME

It's the anvil upon which attitudes and convictions are
hammered out...
where we come to terms with circumstances
and where life makes up its mind.

Charles R. Swindoll

Tough Decision

Author unknown

In the days when an ice cream sundae cost much less, a ten-year-old boy entered a hotel coffee shop and sat at a table. A waitress put a glass of water in front of him.

"How much is an ice cream sundae?"

"Fifty cents," replied the waitress.

The little boy pulled his hand out of his pocket and studied a number of coins in it.

"How much is a dish of plain ice cream?" he inquired.

Some people were now waiting for a table and the waitress was a bit impatient.

"Thirty-five cents," she said brusquely.

The little boy again counted the coins. "I'll have the plain ice cream," he said.

The waitress brought the ice cream, put the bill on the table and walked away. The boy finished the ice cream, paid the cashier and departed. When the waitress came back, she began wiping down the table and then swallowed hard at what she saw. There, placed neatly beside the empty dish, were two nickels and five pennies—her tip.

The Porcelain Teacup

Teresa Maud Sullivan

She had come. I caught just a glimpse of her as I walked out of church after the service. The reception in my father's home took up most of the rest of the day, as people came out of love and respect for a man who had spent his whole life among them in this small New England town, where I had grown up and, with great enthusiasm, had moved away from even before I'd finished college.

It had been a beautiful day, both in terms of the kindness of the townspeople—who had baked casseroles and pastries aplenty—and their heartfelt comments, which had washed over me like a cooling balm upon my heartache. It was a true Indian Summer day of the kind that only northern New England states experience. I grinned, thinking that my father was probably quite pleased with himself. It was so strange, but I had felt his presence since returning home, as though we were carrying on a conversation and just mulling over the day, as we had done on my infrequent visits over the years. When I turned my head, I half expected him to be there.

Later I wandered the house, wondering how I would ever dispose of the decades of memories that went with each and every dear article it held. The only thing of which I felt positive was my mother's collection of china, pottery, and porcelain. These were mine. As a child, I would stand and stare at them behind their wall of glass doors, filling my soul with the beauty of their delicate hues and shapes. I had only a few strong memories of my mother, but the clearest one was of the day we staged a tea party and I had been allowed to choose my favorite pieces. We sat with our tea, deep in conversation and secretive laughter.

Now I sat on the old porch swing, which had seen who knows how many tears and kisses as well as those well-remembered heart-to-heart conversations with my father. The warmth of the day was still with me but was starting to fade in the thin, pale light of Indian Summer when my mind returned to the diminutive woman I had glimpsed earlier in the day at church. Her presence had conjured a memory of the day that taught me the greatest lesson of my life.

My mother died when I was only six years old, and afterward my wonderful grandmother took care of my father and me. Body and soul were lovingly nourished, and I know that I was greatly indulged. I rarely incurred my father's wrath, which in itself I glimpsed infrequently, for he was not a man to suffer fools gladly and always reacted quickly and firmly to any display of ill-mannered behavior.

We had returned from church one warm Sunday when I was about eleven, and I had changed into playclothes to spend the afternoon with a young friend. Our day was given over to fun on the front porch until we were called in for Sunday dinner. While we were engrossed in our play, we caught a glimpse of "Crazy Mary" walking by.

Crazy Mary lived on the outskirts of town in a shack made up of cardboard, tin, and whatever other material would ensure her warmth and protection during the cold New England winters. She prowled the town picking up furniture and all manner of odds and ends that would fit in the converted baby carriage, all rust and rickety wheels, that she pushed everywhere. To our knowledge, she never talked to anyone and would suffer silently the taunts of the town children as she walked to and from her small plot. They were frightened of her, of course, myself included.

My friend and I began a tirade of name-calling directed at the tiny figure as she walked slowly past my porch, pushing her ever-present vehicle in front of her. We were making dreadful noises, mocking her clothing as rags and her shoes as cloven hooves, saying any and all things that came to our young minds. There was no fear in us that day, for our victim never lifted her head, and we were secure in the fact that the safety of home surrounded us.

When Crazy Mary had passed out of sight, we convulsed into laughter and collapsed onto the front porch swing. At that moment I saw my father standing there, with a look I could not fathom, but I could sense his anger. In a quiet yet controlled voice he sent my friend home, then turned to me and ordered me to go to my room, wash up, and put on the dress I had worn to church that morning. I did not understand his intent, but knowing my father, any questions on my part would only incur more of his disapproval. I never opened my mouth.

When I returned to the porch, where my father was sitting with my grandmother, her look of grave disapproval only heightened my fear. He told me that we were going for a walk, and along the way I was to think of what I would say to "Miss Mary" in way of apology for my rudeness and lack of civility and manners. I have no idea how far it was that we walked that day. My mind was a whirl of words, but I could not call them into order, and when we stopped at that dreadful destination, my father looked long and hard at me, then motioned for me to approach the door.

The familiar figure opened what passed for a door, and my father uncovered his head and announced that we had come to call. The woman, clothed so poorly, stepped aside and my father and I entered. The darkness after the sunlight rendered me almost sightless, and the first thing that assailed me was the coolness of that room and the faint odor of damp earth. When my eyes adjusted I saw that she was moving around to find seats for us. My father told her with a smile that before we could accept her hospitality, his daughter had something to say, and he turned to me. To this day I cannot recall what I said; my throat was bone-dry, but whatever words tumbled out, they evidently satisfied my father, and our hostess looked at me and softly said "Thank you."

We sat then, and as she bustled around that small room with only one small window for light, I could see that she was preparing a tea tray. She and my father joined in light conversation, and when she turned my father rose and took the tray from her as she indicated for him to place it on the only table in the room. She served us our tea. When she handed the teacup and saucer to me I was dumbstruck. I looked down at the exquisite china that rested on my palm, and I could not believe my eyes: The delicacy and colors of that china so moved me that tears started from my eyes and down my face. The only thought that came to mind was of my mother—she must be like my mother! The woman got up from her chair and came over to me. She gave me a biscuit and at the same time she wiped away my tears and smiled at me. Polite conversation resumed, and my father told her how I was following in my mother's footsteps by fast becoming a china buff, which would have pleased my mother immensely.

I never said a word. I just stared at the two of them. In due time, but acting with unhurried grace, my father rose, thanked her for the hospitality of her home, and turned to me. She quickly took my cup and, going over to her washbasin, she rinsed and dried it, came back to me and took my hand, and placed the cup and saucer in it. She smiled, said "For you," and opened the door for our leave-taking. My feet felt rooted, and I stood unmoving. At last I found my tongue, and I was able to say with a tear-strained voice, "It's beautiful—thank you."

The walk back home was silent, for I was filled with confusion, and my father did not intrude upon that silence. I went straight to my room and sat staring out my window and thinking of the teacup: Had she known my mother? Had she been a friend to my mother and father long ago? Had she suffered some terrible loss that made her so lonely now?

It was to be years before the full impact of that day would settle in my brain. I had been taught a lesson that would be with me for the rest of my life: The worth of a human being is priceless and the power of the human spirit must be prized and respected above all things.

My father and I never discussed that day again. If he knew anything about Miss Mary's past, he never shared the information with me—and I never asked him to. It was enough that I had redeemed myself in his eyes—and in hers.

Home is a place where we find direction.

Gigi Graham Tchividjian

The Little Town Is Where...

Paul Harvey

As often as convenient, the Harveys may be found at our hideaway farm in the Missouri Ozarks.

Nothing fancy, believe me.

Rolling hills of mostly oak trees. Patch pastures.

Family orchard. House garden.

And in season, chiggers.

The nearest town is not one whose name you'd know.

A long time ago the Cushing, Oklahoma, *Daily Citizen* tried to explain the charm of the "little town." I rewrote what they wrote about theirs—to fit ours.

A little town is where everybody knows what everybody else is doing—but they read the weekly newspaper to see who got caught at it.

In a little town everybody knows every neighbor's car by sight and most by sound—and also knows when it comes and where it goes.

In a little town there's no use anybody lyin' about his age or his ailments or exaggerating about his ancestors or his offspring.

A little town is where, if you get the wrong number, you can talk for 15 minutes anyway— if you want to.

A little town is where there's hardly anything to do and never enough time to do it.

In any town the ratio of good people to bad people is a hundred to one.

In a big town, the hundred are uncomfortable.

In a little town, the "one" is.

A little town is where businessmen struggle for survival against suburban shopping centers...

Where they dig deep to support anybody's worthy cause, though they know "anybody" shops mostly at city stores.

Small-town gossip tends to cut down anybody who's up, help up anybody who's down.

The small-town policeman has a first name.

The small-town schoolteacher has the last word.

The small-town preacher is a full-time farmer.

The small-town firemen take turns.

Why would anybody want to live in one of these tiny "blink-and-you-miss-it-towns"?

I don't know. Maybe because in the class play there's a part for everybody.

In the town jail there's rarely anybody.

In the town cemetery, you're still among friends.

The Toolbox

Joshua Harris
from I Kissed Dating Goodbye

Recently my dad and my younger brother Joel attended a birthday party for Stephen Taylor, one of Joel's best friends. It was a very special occasion. Stephen was turning thirteen, and his dad wanted to make Stephen's entrance into young adulthood memorable. Nice presents wouldn't suffice; Stephen's dad wanted to impart wisdom. To accomplish this he asked fathers to accompany their sons to the party and to bring a special gift—a tool that served them in their specific lines of work.

Each father gave his tool to Stephen along with its accompanying "life lesson" for the "toolbox" of principles Stephen would carry into life. The tools were as unique as the men who used them. My dad gave Stephen a quality writing pen and explained that a pen not only served him when he wrote his ideas but also represented his word when he signed an agreement.

During the gift giving, a father who was a professional home builder handed Stephen a small box. "Inside that box is the tool I use most," he said. Stephen opened it and found a nail puller.

"My nail puller, simple as it might seem," the father explained, "is one of the most important tools I have." This father told the story of how once, while in the middle of building a wall, he discovered that it was crooked. Instead of halting the construction and undoing a little work to fix the wall, he decided to proceed, hoping that the problem would go away as he continued to build. However, the problem only worsened. Eventually, at a great loss of materials and time, he had to tear down the nearly completed wall and totally rebuild it.

"Stephen," the father said gravely, "times will come in life when you'll realize you've made a mistake. At that moment, you have two choices: You can swallow your pride and 'pull a few nails,' or you can foolishly continue your course, hoping the problem will go away. Most of the time the problem will only get worse. I'm giving you this tool to remind you of this principle: When you realize you've made a mistake, the best thing you can do is tear it down and start over."

Children are a great deal more apt to follow your lead than the way you point.

Author unknown

Contentment

Ruth Senter
from Have We Really Come a Long Way?

hat do you want for Christmas?" I ask. It's October and I'm already into a semi-panic about my shopping list.

"I don't know," she answers simply. "I have everything I need."

I am not so easily put off.

"Come on, Mother. You must need *something.*"

She is immovable.

"No. I really don't."

And she actually means it. As far as she is concerned, she has all she needs.

I look around her house. She could use new carpet in the room she and Daddy affectionately refer to as "The Study." It is their private sanctuary—barely big enough for their two recliners, Daddy's big oak desk (which has been around since before time began), a small two-drawer file painted light green to match the walls, and a bookshelf creatively housed in a closet with the doors removed so it looks like part of the room.

The room is appropriately dubbed "The Study" because it's where Daddy studies and prepares his sermons and where he and Mother study their Bible every morning without fail.

The Study is also the platform from which they study the birds, the clouds, the trees. They've set their recliners so they can keep an eye on the world beyond the plate-glass patio doors.

From The Study they examine the world at large. Every evening after the day's news has been digested they fold the newspaper and slip it into the old magazine rack between their two recliners. The newspapers are carried out to the recycle bin once a week. But until then, their "textbooks" to the world are kept close at hand. You never know what information you may need in the course of the week.

"Yes," says Mother. "I have all I need."

But still, The Study does need new carpet, and for all the entertaining Mother's done, she's never had a soup tureen or ice cream dishes or silver napkin rings.

I tell Mother if she can't think of anything she needs, I will think of something for her. And she is just as happy about that. She pulls out her big cast-iron skillet and begins to brown the chicken for supper. She has no further comment about her needs.

In fact, for as long as I can remember she has not commented about her needs. She simply lives from sunup to sundown, savoring the beauty of the day outside. And if it is raining, she turns on all the lamps in the house and savors the warmth of her cozy rooms. In between the savoring, she tells me how good God is, how fortunate she is to be married to Daddy, and how wonderful her children are. (No wonder I like to go home.)

True, my mother has her down times just like everyone else. She has walked through many a valley. But I have seen contentment so spelled out in the life of my mother that I could not create the quality in a character more completely were I writing fiction. I get the feeling Mother is content with what she has in the way of material possessions. But there is something even deeper. I sense she is content with who she is and what she does.

Being with my mother always arouses a certain sad nostalgia. I am not wishing back my childhood, as warm and nurturing as it was. But I *am* wishing back the contentment I find in my mother. I wish it for myself. I wish it for women everywhere who seem so restless, so filled with longing.

Sometimes I wonder about this old-fashioned brand of serenity I saw in my great-grandma and see today in my mother.

I cannot say for sure exactly what it was. Certainly, it had to do with their walk with God. With their strength of character. But I suspect it also had something to do with their belief that they were significant.

PIECE BY PIECE

Good character is more to be praised than outstanding talent.
Most talents are, to some extent, a gift.
Good character, by contrast, is not given to us.
We have to build it piece by piece—
By thought, choice, courage and determination.

John Luther

Breaking Old Habits

Charles R. Swindoll
from Living Above the Level of Mediocrity

In our nation of fast foods and quick fixes, the great hope of Americans is overnight change. Many are too impatient to wait for anything and too lazy to work long and hard to make it happen. We want what we want when we want it, and the sooner the better—which explains our constant pursuit of hurry-up formulas. Everything from diet fads promising rapid weight loss to immediate financial success through clever schemes captures our fancy and gets our vote.

All this reminds me of a funny story I heard recently. A fellow was raised in the back hills of West Virginia—I mean, so far out in the sticks, never in his life had he even seen a big city, to say nothing of modern inventions and neon lights. He married a gal just like himself and they spent all their married years in the backwoods. They had one son, whom they creatively named Junior. Around the time Junior reached his sixteenth birthday, his dad began to realize it wouldn't be too many years before their son would become a man and would strike out on his own. It troubled him that his boy could reach manhood and wind up getting a job in the city, not prepared to face the real world. He felt responsible and decided to do something about it.

He and his wife started saving for a trip the three of them would take to the city. About three years later the big day arrived. They tossed their belongings in the ol' pickup and started the long journey over winding, rough roads to the city. Their plan was to spend several days at a swanky hotel and take in all the sights. As they approached the outskirts of the metropolis, Papa began to get a little jumpy: "Mama, when we pull up at th' hotel, you stay in th' truck while Junior an' I go in an' look around. We'll come back and git ya, okay?" She agreed.

Flashing neon lights and uniformed doormen greeted them as they pulled up. Mama stayed put as Papa and Junior walked wide-eyed toward the lobby. Neither could believe his eyes! When they stepped on a mat, the doors opened automatically. Inside, they stood like statues, staring at the first chandelier either of them had ever seen. It hung from a ceiling three stories high. Off to the left was an enormous waterfall, rippling over inlaid stones and rocks. "Junior, look!" Papa was pointing toward a long mall where busy shoppers were going in and out of beautiful stores. "Papa, looka there!" Down below was an ice-skating rink—*inside.*

While both stood silent, watching one breathtaking sight after another, they kept hearing a clicking sound behind them. Finally, Papa turned around and saw this amazing little room with doors that slid open from the center. "What in the world?" People would walk up, push a button and wait. Lights would flicker above the doors and then, "click," the doors would slide open from the middle. Some people would walk out of the little room and others would walk inside and turn around as, "click," the doors slid shut. By now, dad and son stood *totally* transfixed.

At that moment a wrinkled old lady shuffled up to the doors all by herself. She pushed the button and waited only a few seconds. "Click," the doors opened with a swish and she hobbled into the little room. No one else stepped in with her, so "click," the doors slid shut. No more than twenty seconds later the doors opened again—and there stood this fabulously attractive blonde, a young woman in her twenties—high heels, shapely body, beautiful face—a real knockout! As she stepped out, smiled, and turned to walk away, Papa nudged his boy and mumbled, "Hey, Junior...*go git Mama!*"

Seems like everybody these days is looking for a room like

what Papa thought he had found. Just push the right button, wait momentarily for the door of opportunity to slide open, then "click," magic! In only a matter of seconds we are instantly transformed. Whom are we kidding? That makes a pretty good joke, but when it comes to reality, nothing could be further from the truth. This is especially true when it comes to the cultivation of character. Honestly, I know of nothing that takes longer, is harder work, or requires greater effort than breaking the old habits that hold us in the grip of mediocrity. No eagle instantly or automatically soars!

I have found three things most inhibit my happiness—
Judgment of others
Negative thoughts
Envy

from PS I Love You

Me 'n Ronnie

Charlie W. Shedd
from Letters to My Grandchildren

That evening, Philip came storming into the house, mad.
You're right. "Angry" is the word. But this boy was
"mad, mad, mad."

Of course, it was Ronnie's fault again. Ronnie lived across
the street and he was Philip's buddy. But, no sir, not this time.
Whatever he'd done, Ronnie could never come into our house
again. Never. Never.

So we ate our meal somewhat subdued that night.
Somewhat sad. We like Ronnie. Fact is, we loved him.

Then suddenly, the doorbell rang. Philip, as usual, ran to
answer and here he came...with whom? You guessed it.

"Hey, Mom, can Ronnie have some ice cream too?"

"Of course, he can. But Philip, what about all those things
you were saying? Didn't you mean them?"

"Oh, sure," came the answer, "I meant them. But me 'n
Ronnie, we got good forgetters."

Wouldn't it be wonderful if every one of us could say that?
And mean it?

Courageous Choices

Tim Kimmel
from Raising Kids Who Turn Out Right

T wo people immediately come to mind when I think about preparing our kids to make courageous choices. Jerry and Cheryl are parents of three beautiful daughters. Their girls have been the beneficiaries of a loving and stable spiritual environment. But even with all this godly teaching and understanding, with all this love and security, Jerry and Cheryl knew that without courage their daughters could easily fall to outside pressures.

Just about the time their oldest daughter, Shelly, blossomed into a beautiful young woman, they decided to do something memorable to help her maintain courage. It was easy for them to develop a plan because they knew what character traits they were trying to encourage.

They took some of their own gold jewelry, had the jeweler form it into a key, strung the key on a chain, and made it into a necklace. They washed their car, dry-cleaned Jerry's suit, and bought a simple corsage.

Then Jerry took his daughter out on her first "adult" date.

They enjoyed an elegant dinner in one of their town's finest restaurants. During the meal Jerry talked to Shelly about the courage she would need to stay morally pure. When dessert was served, Jerry took out the gift-wrapped jewelry box containing the necklace. But before she put it on, he told her its significance.

The gold symbolized her purity and the key symbolized the key to her heart. She was to wear it as a reminder of the moral purity that God wanted her to bring to her honeymoon bed. Every time she went out on a date, and anytime she might be tempted to compromise her purity, this gold key around her neck was to remind her of God's view of marriage. Then, on the night of her honeymoon, she could take if off and give it to her husband. With it she could let him know that she had pre-served her purity as a gift for him.

Maybe that's why I like Jerry and Cheryl so much. They realize that courage doesn't come easy; but regardless of its cost, it must be transferred to their children.

GOOD ADVICE

God sees everything and hears everything and is everywhere,
which keeps Him pretty busy.
So you shouldn't go wasting His time
by going over your parent's head
asking for something they said you couldn't have.

Danny Dutton, age 8

Rules for Living

Author unknown

If you open it, close it.
If you turn it on, turn it off.
If you unlock it, lock it up.
If you break it, admit it.
If you can't fix it, call in someone who can.
If you borrow it, return it.
If you value it, take care of it.
If you make a mess, clean it up.
If you move it, put it back.
If it belongs to someone else and you want to use it,
    get permission.
If you don't know how to operate it, leave it alone.
If it's none of your business, don't ask questions.
If it ain't broke, don't fix it.
If it will brighten someone's day, say it.
If it will tarnish someone's reputation, keep it to yourself.

The Beautiful Wife

Carla Muir

A young girl was sitting with her friend at church on a bright Sunday morning. After preaching a sermon on "having a grateful heart," the pastor asked if people would come forward and share something for which they were thankful. The visiting girl listened intently as people rattled off their blessings. A distinguished man in his late fifties was the last to speak. He bragged on and on about his "beautiful wife." He spoke of her encouraging words, and strong faith in the Lord. He closed by thanking his wife for marrying him thirty-two years ago. There was a roar of "amens" as the congregation agreed that he was indeed fortunate to have married her.

By now the young girl was looking around, trying to figure out who this beautiful, saintly woman was. Since the church was large, she finally gave up and asked her friend if she by chance knew who the wife was. "Oh yes," she replied, "everyone knows her. I'll point her out to you after church." After two more songs and a closing prayer, the service ended. As they slowly made their way up the aisle, her friend pointed and said, "She's over there in the corner." There an attractive woman was standing in a brilliant blue dress, laughing and chatting with a woman who had obviously been in a wheelchair for many years. The woman in the blue dress reached down and gave the smiling, crippled woman a big hug.

"So that's the beautiful wife that man was talking about," observed the young visitor, looking at the woman in her brilliant blue dress. "Yes, it is!" replied her friend, admiring the woman in the wheelchair.

The Little Bent Spoon

Joni Eareckson Tada
from Not One Shall Perish

O nce upon a time there was a kitchen drawer full of knives, forks and spoons." The group of disabled boys and girls, sitting in wheelchairs and leaning on crutches, was fascinated. They could tell this would be no ordinary story.

"Amongst the flatware, there was one spoon all twisted and bent. He didn't look like the others. That's why the spoons in the drawer made fun of him, taunting, 'You're no good... Who's going to use you?!' The little bent spoon couldn't help but feel sad."

As I told the story and looked deep into the eyes of the children with cerebral palsy, sitting bent and twisted in their wheelchairs, I thought I saw a glimmer of empathy. Could they know how the spoon felt?

"The little spoon looked a lot like this one," I said as my friend held up my "spork," a utensil with serrated prongs that someone inserts into my hand splint so I can feed myself. (It's misshapen, but the angle is perfect for lifting food from my plate to my mouth.)

"But one day the drawer opened and a big hand reached inside. Instead of choosing a shiny, straight spoon, the master of the household picked...the ugly bent spoon! The rest of the flatware were amazed. And as the bent spoon was lifted out of the drawer, he beamed with pleasure. He was about to be used by the master."

The boys and girls giggled. They watched my friend place the spork in my hand splint and smiled to see me lift my arm to feed myself. "And children, I wouldn't be able to eat were it not for this special spoon. True, it doesn't look 'normal,' and it doesn't fit in the utensil tray with all the other knives and forks. But there's no way I'll ever want to 'straighten it out.'"

The kids were fascinated. "The important thing to remember is this: The Master loves choosing people who are different to do His good work. Jesus knows He can use us when He bends us to suit His will...He can best use us when we're shaped for His special design."

My friend placed my spork back in my handbag. But the lesson remained of God's love (as well as His purpose!) for boys and girls who look different. A twisted spoon...and the bent body of a child...all have a unique and special purpose when placed in the Master's hand.

The White Handkerchief

Patricia St. John
from Stories to Share

T he man sat on the pavement beside the bus stop and stared at the stones. A few people turned to look at him—his unshaven face, his slumped shoulders, and broken shoes, but he was not aware of their glances because he was reliving his life. He was no longer a hungry tramp who had slept last night under a railway arch; he was a boy who lived in a small red brick house up the next street, more than twenty years ago. Perhaps they had bulldozed over the house by now; he hoped they hadn't crushed the pansies. It was strange how well he could remember the pansies, and the swing his dad had made for him, and the path where he had learned to ride his bike. They had saved up for months to buy that bike.

The man shrugged impatiently, for the brightness of those pictures hurt him, and his memory traveled on another ten years. The bike had been exchanged for a motorcycle, and he had begun to come home less often. He had a job by then and plenty of friends. Mum and Dad seemed a bit sad and gray, and the pubs were a lot more fun. He did not really want to remember those years, nor the day when the debts had piled up and he had gone home meaning to ask for money. They had made him a cup of tea, and he had not liked to mention what he had come for. But he knew exactly where his dad kept the money, and later on, when his parents went out into the garden, it was quite easy to help himself to what he wanted.

That was the last time he had seen them. He had not wanted to go home again after that, and they had lost track of him. He had gone abroad, and they knew nothing about the years of wandering and the prison sentence. But locked in his cell at night he had thought a lot about them. Sometimes when he tossed awake, and the moonlight moved across the wall, he used to wonder. Once free, he would love to see them again, if they were still alive, and always supposing they still wanted to see him.

When his time was up, he found a job in the town, but he could not settle. Something seemed to be drawing him home with an urge he could not get away from. Every time he went for a walk something reminded him—a clump of pansies, a child on a swing, a little boy running home from school—he could not forget the small red brick house.

He did not want to arrive penniless, so he walked or hitchhiked a good deal of the long journey home. He could have arrived earlier, but twenty miles away he was suddenly overcome with misgivings. What right had he to walk in like this? Could they ever reconcile the haggard man he had become with the boy they had loved who had so bitterly disappointed them?

He bought some food and spent most of that day sitting under a tree. The letter he posted that evening was quite short, but it had taken him hours to write. It ended with these words:

> I know it is unreasonable of me to suppose that you want to see me...so it's up to you. I'll come to the end of the road early Thursday morning. If you want me home, hang a white handkerchief in the window of my old bedroom. If it's there, I'll come on; if not, I'll wave good-bye to the old house and go on my way.

And now it was Thursday morning. He had arrived at the end of the street. It was still there! But having got there, he felt in no hurry at all. He just sat down on the pavement and stared at the stones.

Well, he could not put it off forever, and after all they might have moved. If the handkerchief was not there he would make a few inquiries before actually leaving the town. He had not yet had the courage to face what he would do if they were there and simply did not want him.

He got up painfully, for he was stiff from sleeping outside. The street was still in shadow. Shivering a little, he walked slowly toward the old oak tree where he knew he could see the old house as clear as clear. He would not look till he got there.

He stood under the boughs with his eyes shut for a moment. Then he drew a long breath and looked. Then he stood staring.

The sun was already shining on the little red brick house, but it no longer seemed to be a little red brick house, for every wall was festooned with white. Every window was hung with sheets, pillowcases, towels, tablecloths, handkerchiefs, and table napkins; and white muslin curtains trailed across the roof from the attic window. It looked like a snow house gleaming in the morning light.

His parents were taking no risks.

The man threw his head back and gave a cry of relief. Then he ran up the street and straight in at the open front door.

A Good Lesson

Author unknown
Retold by Artin Tellalian

A young man, a student in one of our universities, was one day taking a walk with a professor, who was commonly called the students' friend, from his kindness to those who waited on his instructions. As they went along, they saw lying in the path a pair of old shoes, which they supposed to belong to a poor man who was employed in a field close by, and who had nearly finished his day's work.

The student turned to the professor, saying: "Let us play the man a trick: we will hide his shoes, and conceal ourselves behind those bushes, and wait to see his perplexity when he cannot find them." "My young friend," answered the professor, "we should never amuse ourselves at the expense of the poor. But you are rich, and may give yourself a much greater pleasure by means of this poor man. Put a coin into each shoe, and then we will hide ourselves and watch how the discovery affects him."

The student did so, and they both placed themselves behind the bushes close by. The poor man soon finished his work, and came across the field to the path where he had left his coat and shoes. While putting on his coat he slipped his foot into one of his shoes; but feeling something hard, he stooped down to feel what it was, and found the coin. Astonishment and wonder were seen upon his countenance. He gazed upon the coin, turned it round, and looked at it again and again. He then looked around him on all sides, but no person was to be seen. He now put the money into his pocket, and proceeded to put on the other shoe; but his surprise was doubled on finding the other coin. His feelings overcame him; he fell upon his knees, looked up to heaven and uttered aloud a fervent thanksgiving, in which he spoke of his wife, sick and helpless, and his children without bread, whom this timely bounty, from some unknown hand, would save from perishing.

The student stood there deeply affected, and his eyes filled with tears. "Now," said the professor, "are you not much better pleased than if you had played your intended trick?" The youth replied, "You have taught me a lesson which I will never forget. I feel now the truth of these words, which I never understood before: 'It is more blessed to give than to receive.'"

Kindness

Clark Cothern
from At the Heart of Every Good Father

Ten-year-old Joseph Fisher learned a lesson on kindness when he almost ran over his dad with a tractor. Listen as Joe tells his story.

"I was breaking up some dirt one afternoon while my dad was working on a piece of equipment in the bar ditch on the north side of the field. The old Farmall tractor I was driving had to be turned by pulling a brake on one rear wheel or the other. If you applied the brake to the left wheel, the right wheel kept turning, so naturally, the tractor turned left. If you pulled the right brake, you turned right. It seems so obvious, but when you're ten...you sometimes forget these basic instructions.

"My dad was seated on the opposite side of the ditch, directly in front of where I was headed, and he was intent on his work, so he didn't see the big double wheels of the tractor until I pulled the wrong brake and started the tractor sliding in the wrong direction.

"I almost panicked, trying to stop the big old thing, but my dad jumped out of the way at the last minute, and the heavy front end of the tractor thumped to a stop right where Dad had been sitting.

"I expected him to come clean my plow (and not on the tractor), so I sat with my hands on the wheel, bracing myself for the explosion. Instead, he calmly walked up to me and asked, 'Are you okay?'

"I couldn't believe it. Here I was sitting on this huge tractor that I had almost steered right over my dad, and he asked if I was okay! When I told him I was fine, he simply said, 'Well, good. Do you know what you did wrong?' I told him, 'Yes sir,' and he said, 'Great. There's a lesson you won't soon forget.' And he just smiled, patted my knee, and watched me drive the tractor back onto the field. Then he climbed back into the ditch and went back to work."

When You Thought I Wasn't Looking

Mary Rita Schilke Korzan

When you thought I wasn't looking you hung my first painting on the refrigerator, and I wanted to paint another.

When you thought I wasn't looking you fed a stray cat, and I thought it was good to be kind to animals.

When you thought I wasn't looking you baked a birthday cake just for me, and I knew that little things were special things.

When you thought I wasn't looking you said a prayer, and I believed there was a God that I could always talk to.

When you thought I wasn't looking you kissed me goodnight, and I felt loved.

When you thought I wasn't looking I saw tears come from your eyes, and I learned that sometimes things hurt—but that it's all right to cry.

When you thought I wasn't looking you smiled, and it made me want to look that pretty, too.

When you thought I wasn't looking you cared, and I wanted to be everything I could be.

When you thought I wasn't looking—I looked...and wanted to say thanks for all those things you did when you thought I wasn't looking.

Growing Up

SOMEDAY THEY WILL FLY

I see children as kites. You spend a lifetime trying to get them off the ground. You run with them until you're both breathless...they crash...you add a longer tail. You patch and comfort, adjust and teach—and assure them that someday they will fly.

Finally they are airborne, but they need more string, and you keep letting it out...You know it won't be long before that beautiful creature will snap the lifeline that bound you together and soar—free and alone. Only then do you know you did your job.

Erma Bombeck
from Forever Erma

Our Girl

Max Lucado
from Six Hours One Friday

J enna, wake up. It's time to go to school."
She will hear those words a thousand times in her life. But she heard them for the first time this morning.

I sat on the edge of her bed for a while before I said them to her. To tell the truth, I didn't want to say them. I didn't want to wake her. A queer hesitancy hung over me as I sat in the early morning blackness. As I sat in silence, I realized that my words would awaken her to a new world.

For four lightning-fast years she'd been ours, and ours alone. And now that was all going to change.

We put her to bed last night as "our girl"—exclusive property of Mommy and Daddy. Mommy and Daddy read to her, taught her, listened to her. But beginning today, someone else would, too.

Until today, it was Mommy and Daddy who wiped away the tears and put on the Band-Aids. But beginning today, someone else would, too.

I didn't want to wake her.

Until today, her life was essentially us—Mom, Dad, and baby sister Andrea. Today that life would grow—new friends, a teacher. Her world was this house—her room, her toys, her swing set. Today her world would expand. She would enter the winding halls of education—painting, reading, calculating... becoming.

I didn't want to wake her. Not because of the school. It's a fine one. Not because I don't want her to learn. Heaven knows I want her to grow, to read, to mature. Not because she doesn't want to go. School has been all she could talk about for the last week!

No, I didn't want to wake her up because I didn't want to give her up.

But I woke her anyway. I interrupted her childhood with the inevitable proclamation, "Jenna, wake up—it's time to go to school."

It took me forever to get dressed. Denalyn saw me moping around and heard me humming, "Sunrise, Sunset" and said, "You'll never make it through her wedding." She's right.

We took her to school in two cars so that I could go directly to work. I asked Jenna to ride with me. I thought I should give her a bit of fatherly assurance. As it turned out, I was the one needing assurance.

For one dedicated to the craft of words, I found very few to share with her. I told her to enjoy herself. I told her to obey her teacher. I told her, "If you get lonely or afraid, tell your teacher to call me and I'll come and get you." "Okay," she smiled. Then she asked if she could listen to a tape with kids' music. "Okay," I said.

So while she sang songs, I swallowed lumps. I watched her as she sang. She looked big. Her little neck stretched as high as it could to look over the dash. Her eyes were hungry and bright. Her hands were folded in her lap. Her feet, wearing brand new turquoise and pink tennis shoes, barely extended over the seat....

Sunrise, sunset; sunrise, sunset;
Swiftly fly the days. [1]

"Denalyn was right," I mumbled to myself. "I'll never make it through the wedding."

What is she thinking? I wondered. *Does she know how tall this ladder of education is that she will begin climbing this morning?*

No, she didn't. But I did. How many chalkboards will those eyes see? How many books will those hands hold? How many teachers will those feet follow and—gulp—imitate?

Were it within my power, I would have, at that very instant, assembled all the hundreds of teachers, instructors, coaches, and tutors that she would have over the next eighteen years and announced, "This is no normal student. This is my child. Be careful with her!"

As I parked and turned off the engine, my big girl became small again. But it was a voice of a very little girl that broke the silence. "Daddy, I don't want to get out."

I looked at her. The eyes that had been bright were now fearful. The lips that had been singing were now trembling.

I fought a Herculean urge to grant her request. Everything within me wanted to say, "Okay, let's forget it and get out of here." For a brief, eternal moment I considered kidnapping my own daughters, grabbing my wife, and escaping these horrid paws of progress to live forever in the Himalayas.

But I knew better. I knew it was time. I knew it was right. And I knew she would be fine. But I never knew it would be so hard to say, "Honey, you'll be all right. Come on, I'll carry you."

And she *was* all right. One step into the classroom and the cat of curiosity pounced on her. And I walked away. I gave her up. Not much. And not as much as I will have to in the future. But I gave her up as much as I could today.

1. "Sunrise, Sunset" (Jerry Bock, Sheldon Harnick), © 1964—Alley Music Corp. and Trio Music Co. Inc.

A Great Cup of Tea

James Dobson
from Home with a Heart

I heard a story about a mother who was sick in bed with the flu. Her darling daughter wanted so much to be a good nurse. She fluffed the pillows and brought a magazine for her mother to read. And then she even showed up with a surprise cup of tea.

"Why, you're such a sweetheart," the mother said as she drank the tea. "I didn't know you even knew how to make tea."

"Oh, yes," the little girl replied. "I learned by watching you. I put the tea leaves in the pan and then I put in the water, and I boiled it, and then I strained it into a cup. But I couldn't find a strainer, so I used the flyswatter instead."

"You what?" the mother screamed.

And the little girl said, "Oh, don't worry, Mom, I didn't use the new flyswatter. I used the old one."

No More Oatmeal Kisses

Erma Bombeck
from Forever Erma

A young mother writes: "I know you've written before about the empty-nest syndrome, that lonely period after the children are grown and gone. Right now I'm up to my eyeballs in laundry and muddy boots. The baby is teething; the boys are fighting. My husband just called and said to eat without him, and I fell off my diet. Lay it on me again, will you?"

OK. One of these days, you'll shout, "Why don't you kids grow up and act your age!" And they will. Or, "You guys get outside and find yourselves something to do...and don't slam the door!" And they won't.

You'll straighten up the boys' bedroom neat and tidy: bumper stickers discarded, bedspread tucked and smooth, toys displayed on the shelves. Hangers in the closet. Animals caged. And you'll say out loud, "Now I want it to stay this way." And it will.

You'll prepare a perfect dinner with a salad that hasn't been picked to death and a cake with no finger traces in the icing, and you'll say, "Now, there's a meal for company." And you'll eat it alone.

You'll say, "I want complete privacy on the phone. No dancing around. No demolition crews. Silence! Do you hear?" And you'll have it.

No more plastic tablecloths stained with spaghetti. No more bedspreads to protect the sofa from damp bottoms. No more gates to stumble over at the top of the basement steps. No more clothespins under the sofa. No more playpens to arrange a room around.

No more anxious nights under a vaporizer tent. No more

sand on the sheets or Popeye movies in the bathroom. No more iron-on patches, rubber bands for ponytails, tight boots or wet knotted shoestrings.

Imagine. A lipstick with a point on it. No baby-sitter for New Year's Eve. Washing only once a week. Seeing a steak that isn't ground. Having your teeth cleaned without a baby on your lap.

No PTA meetings. No car pools. No blaring radios. No one washing her hair at 11 o'clock at night. Having your own roll of Scotch tape.

Think about it. No more Christmas presents out of toothpicks and library paste. No more sloppy oatmeal kisses. No more tooth fairy. No more giggles in the dark. No knees to heal, no responsibility.

Only a voice crying, "Why don't you grow up?" and the silence echoing, "I did."

PRIVILEGED INFORMATION

After living in large cities all their lives,
my daughter's family moved to our rural community.
Driving home one evening, she pointed out a big rabbit.
"Look kids. It's a jackrabbit," her husband said.
After everyone quieted down again, their four-year-old said,
"Wow, Daddy, do you know all the rabbits' names?"

Pearl Conaway
from A Woman's Touch *magazine*

My Two Sons

Melody Carlson

My two sons,
I always wanted you.
Even when I was a little girl
Playing with baby dolls.
I clothed them and fed them,
Rocked them and sang a lullaby.
Thinking that one day,
I would have babes of my own.

And God gave me you,
My two sons.
And I clothed you and fed you,
I rocked you to sleep
And sang you a lullaby.
And it was wonderful.
I wanted it to last
Forever.

But quickly you grew older,
With sturdy legs and grinning faces.
And we made a sandbox,
Played with Legos,
And read stories.
We learned to ride bikes,
And mended owies.
And you grew up.

Now you are young men.
Both over six feet tall,
with whiskers.
It feels like you don't need me—
very much.
And I have to let go.
And trust God to care for you,
But it's the hardest thing I've ever done.

My two sons,
I always wanted you.
But now all *I* can do
Is watch and pray,
That you will let God
Clothe you, and feed you,
Rock you and sing you a lullaby.
And it will be wonderful.

The Ring Bearer

Dennis Kizziar
Retold by Matt Jacobson

J ohnny was very excited. It was the first time he had ever been asked to do something this important. As the wedding music began to play he imagined just how he should carry the pillow with two shiny rings tied on top. Just before touching him on the shoulder to give him the cue to walk down the aisle, his mother looked down and smiled into the upturned face of her four-year-old son. "Don't worry, Mommy." Johnny implored, "I'll do a good job."

Then Johnny took a deep breath, furrowed his brow, bared his teeth and said Grrrrrrr! Everyone turned to face the back of the church. Where was that strange noise coming from?

Johnny growled all the louder and much to Mrs. Smith's surprise, who was sitting on the third pew from the back, he ran up to her and struck her feathered hat with the pillow. His mother looked on in horror. Johnny was fast. He ran back and forth from pew to pew growling and making menacing faces.

Upon reaching the front of the church, Johnny composed himself and gently held up the pillow so the pastor, nonplused at the performance, could remove the rings. The rest of the ceremony went off without a hitch.

During the reception, the pastor walked up to Johnny who was getting his second piece of wedding cake. "Say, Johnny, what were you doing while bringing the rings to me?"

"My job," declared Johnny proudly, "They asked me to be the Ring Bear!"

A Mother's Letter to a Son Starting Kindergarten

Rebecca Christian

Dear George,
    When your big brother and your little dog and I walked you up to school today, you had no idea how I was feeling.

You were so excited, you had packed and unpacked the washable markers and safety scissors in your backpack a dozen times.

I am really going to miss those lazy mornings when we waved your brother and sister off to school. I'd settle in with my coffee and newspaper, handing you the comics to color while you watched *Sesame Street*.

Because you are my youngest, I had learned a few things by the time you came along. I found out that the seemingly endless days of babyhood are gone like lightning. I blinked, and your older siblings were setting off for school as eagerly as you did this morning.

I was one of the lucky ones; I could choose whether to work or not. By the time it was your turn, the glittering prizes of career advancement and a double income had lost their luster. A splash in the puddles with you in your bright red boots or "just one more" rereading of your favorite book, *Frog and Toad Are Friends*, meant more.

You didn't go to preschool and I'm not exactly Maria Montessori. I hope that doesn't hold you back. You learned numbers by helping me count the soda cans we returned to the store. (You could usually charm me into letting you pick out a treat with the money we got back.)

I'm not up on the Palmer method, but you do a fine job of

writing your name on the sidewalk in chalk, in capitals to make it look more important. And somehow you caught on to the nuances of language. Just the other day, you asked me why I always call you "Honey" when we're reading stories and "Bud" when you're helping with the chores. My explanation of the difference between a cuddly mood and a matey one seemed to satisfy you.

I have to admit that in my mind's eye, an image of myself while you're in school has developed. I see myself updating all the photo albums and starting that novel I always wanted to write. As the summer wound down and more frequent quarrels erupted between you and your siblings, I was looking forward to today.

And then this morning, I walked you up the steep hill to your classroom with a picture of the president on one wall and of Bambi on the opposite. You found the coat hook with your name above it right away, and you gave me one of your characteristically fierce, too-tight hugs. This time you were ready to let go before I was.

Maybe someday you will deliver a kindergartner with your own wide-set eyes and sudden grin to the first day of school. When you turn at the door to wave good-bye, he or she will be too deep in conversation with a new friend to notice. Even as you smile, you'll feel something warm on your cheek...

And then, you'll know.

Love,
Mom

Just in Case

Tony Campolo
from What My Parents Did Right

L iving as we did in a congested and bustling city, my mother
arranged with a teenage girl who lived next door to walk me
home at the end of the day. For this arduous responsibility,
the girl was paid five cents a day, or a grand total of a quarter a
week. In second grade, I became irritated that our poor family was
giving this neighbor girl so much money, and I offered a deal to
my mom. "Look," I said, "I'll walk myself to school and, if you
give me a nickel a week, I will be extra careful. You can keep the
other twenty cents and we'll all be better off." I pleaded and
begged, and eventually my mother gave in to my proposal. For the
next two years I walked to and from school all by myself. It was an
eight-block walk with many streets to cross, but I crossed them all
with great care. I didn't talk to any strangers. I always kept on the
appointed path. I always did as I promised and I did it alone—or
at least I thought I did.

Years later when we were enjoying a family party, I bragged
about my characteristic independence and, in a grandiose fashion,
reminded my family of how I had been able to take care of myself
even as a small boy. I recalled the arrangements for going to and
from school that I had worked out with Mom. It was then that my
mother laughed and told me the whole story. "Did you really think
you were alone?" she asked. "Every morning when you left for
school, I left with you. I walked behind you all the way. When you
got out of school at 3:30 in the afternoon, I was there. I always
kept myself hidden, but I was there and I followed you all the way
home. I just wanted to be there for you in case you needed me.

Mom *was* always there for me....

The Lovesick Father

A modern setting of the parable in Luke 15:1–32

Philip Yancey
from What's So Amazing about Grace?

A young girl grows up on a cherry orchard just above Traverse City, Michigan. Her parents, a bit old-fashioned, tend to overreact to her nose ring, the music she listens to, and the length of her skirts. They ground her a few times, and she seethes inside. "I hate you!" she screams at her father when he knocks on the door of her room after an argument, and that night she acts on a plan she has mentally rehearsed scores of times. She runs away.

She has visited Detroit only once before, on a bus trip with her church youth group to watch the Tigers play. Because newspapers in Traverse City report in lurid detail the gangs, the drugs, and the violence in downtown Detroit, she concludes that this is probably the last place her parents will look for her. California, maybe, or Florida, but not Detroit.

Her second day there she meets a man who drives the biggest car she's ever seen. He offers her a ride, buys her lunch, arranges a place for her to stay. He gives her some pills that make her feel better than she's ever felt before. She was right all along, she decides: her parents were keeping her from all the fun.

The good life continues for a month, two months, a year. The man with the big car—she calls him "Boss"—teaches her a few things that men like. Since she's underage, men pay a premium for her. She lives in a penthouse, and orders room service whenever she wants. Occasionally she thinks about the folks back home, but their lives now seem so boring and provincial that she can hardly believe she grew up there.

She has a brief scare when she sees her picture printed on the back of a milk carton with the headline "Have you seen this child?" But by now she has blonde hair, and with all the makeup and body-piercing jewelry she wears, nobody would mistake her for a child. Besides, most of her friends are runaways, and nobody squeals in Detroit.

After a year the first sallow signs of illness appear, and it amazes her how fast the boss turns mean. "These days, we can't mess around," he growls, and before she knows it she's out on the street without a penny to her name. She still turns a couple of tricks a night, but they don't pay much, and all the money goes to support her habit. When winter blows in she finds herself sleeping on metal grates outside the big department stores. "Sleeping" is the wrong word—a teenage girl at night in downtown Detroit can never relax her guard. Dark bands circle her eyes. Her cough worsens.

One night as she lies awake listening for footsteps, all of a sudden everything about her life looks different. She no longer feels like a woman of the world. She feels like a little girl, lost in a cold and frightening city. She begins to whimper. Her pockets are empty and she's hungry. She needs a fix. She pulls her legs tight underneath her and shivers under the newspapers she's piled atop her coat. Something jolts a synapse of memory and a single image fills her mind: of May in Traverse City, when a million cherry trees bloom at once, with her golden retriever dashing through the rows and rows of blossomy trees in chase of a tennis ball.

God, why did I leave, she says to herself, and pain stabs at her heart. *My dog back home eats better than I do now.* She's sobbing, and she knows in a flash that more than anything else in the world she wants to go home.

Three straight phone calls, three straight connections with the answering machine. She hangs up without leaving a message the first two times, but the third time she says, "Dad,

Mom, it's me. I was wondering about maybe coming home. I'm catching a bus up your way, and it'll get there about midnight tomorrow. If you're not there, well, I guess I'll just stay on the bus until it hits Canada."

It takes about seven hours for a bus to make all the stops between Detroit and Traverse City, and during that time she realizes the flaws in her plan. What if her parents are out of town and miss the message? Shouldn't she have waited another day or so until she could talk to them? And even if they are home, they probably wrote her off as dead long ago. She should have given them some time to overcome the shock.

Her thoughts bounce back and forth between those worries and the speech she is preparing for her father. "Dad, I'm sorry. I know I was wrong. It's not your fault; it's all mine. Dad, can you forgive me?" She says the words over and over, her throat tightening even as she rehearses them. She hasn't apologized to anyone in years.

The bus has been driving with lights on since Bay City. Tiny snowflakes hit the pavement rubbed worn by thousands of tires, and the asphalt steams. She's forgotten how dark it gets at night out here. A deer darts across the road and the bus swerves. Every so often, a billboard. A sign posting the mileage to Traverse City. *Oh, God.*

When the bus finally rolls into the station, its air brakes hissing in protest, the driver announces in a crackly voice over the microphone, "Fifteen minutes, folks. That's all we have here." Fifteen minutes to decide her life. She checks herself in a compact mirror, smoothes her hair, and licks the lipstick off her teeth. She looks at the tobacco stains on her fingertips, and wonders if her parents will notice. If they're here.

She walks into the terminal not knowing what to expect. Not one of the thousand scenes that have played out in her mind prepare her for what she sees. There, in the concrete-walls-and-plastic-chairs bus terminal in Traverse City,

Michigan, stands a group of forty brothers and sisters and great-aunts and uncles and cousins and a grandmother and great-grandmother to boot. They're all wearing goofy party hats and blowing noise-makers, and taped across the entire wall of the terminal is a computer-generated banner that reads "Welcome home!"

Out of the crowd of well-wishers breaks her Dad. She stares out through the tears quivering in her eyes like hot mercury and begins the memorized speech, "Dad, I'm sorry. I know...."

He interrupts her. "Hush, child. We've got no time for that. No time for apologies. You'll be late for the party. A banquet's waiting for you at home."

One day, as we were walking through the only mall in our hometown, I suddenly felt the leather of his letterman's jacket as he put his arm around me. Oh, my. My teenage son with his arm around me in public. "Dad, I just want you to know that I love you, that I am so proud to have you as my dad." Everything I had given up ten years earlier could never have meant as much as the sound of those words."

Chuck Miller
from What's Dad Doing Home So Much?

He Never Missed a Game

Robert H. Schuller
from Tough Minded Faith for Tender Hearted People

The story is told of a boy who always had to settle for second-string position. Yet his father never missed a game. After his father's death, the son, with tears in his eyes, said, "Coach, please let me start tonight. I want to play for Dad."

The coach, knowing that the boy's dad had never missed a game, agreed. The young man's performance on the field astounded the coach. When asked to explain his phenomenal level of achievement, he said, "Coach, I played that one for Dad. My father never missed a game, but he never saw me play—until tonight! You see, Coach, my father was blind."

Annie Lee's Gift

Glenda Smithers

Christmas had begun its countdown. At this time of the year Mrs. Stone admitted to only partial control of her students. It was amazing how such a lovely holiday could turn her well-disciplined students into spirited, noisy elves.

"Mrs. Stone, I spilled glue down my new pants," whined Chris.

"Mrs. Stone, my paper chain won't fit around the tree," complained Faye.

"Danielle is flicking paint everywhere!" squealed a girl from the sink area.

Where were her organized lessons and normal routine? And where was her peace of mind? They seemed to have taken a long recess. This recess, Mrs. Stone feared, would last until mid-January.

"Teacher?" A child's voice called from the activity table. Stepping over scraps of paper decorating the carpet, Mrs. Stone moved to where a few children were finishing their calendars for their parent's Christmas gifts.

"Yes, Annie Lee?" asked Mrs. Stone.

The little girl tossed back long, shining hair and answered politely. "Uh...if I finish my calendar, could I take it home tonight? My mother wants to see it. She might have to go—"

"No, Annie Lee," responded Mrs. Stone automatically. "You may take it home on Friday like everybody else."

Annie Lee started to protest but the teacher moved quickly from the table, preoccupied with brushing silver glitter from her skirt.

The Little Drummer Boy's pa-rum-pa-pum-pum suddenly

vibrated the room. "Lavenia, please turn off the record player!" To the rest of the class Mrs. Stone announced, "All right, boys and girls, it's time to clean up."

"Ahhh...." The expected groans of disappointment came and went.

At her desk, Mrs. Stone opened the lid to a small wooden chest and "Silent Night" was immediately recognized by the children. A quiet mood settled over the room as they listened.

"Shay, would you begin our show and tell today?" Mrs. Stone asked while closing the music box. The boy came to the front of the room and said with a slight boast, "I'm getting a red bike for Christmas."

Mrs. Stone closed her eyes. *Here we go again*, she thought. *"I want this and I want that."*

Annie Lee was next to share. Her long hair reflected the sunshine coming through the window as she came forward.

"My mother is sick and can't make the cookies for our party on Friday," she announced.

Mrs. Stone's eyes flew open. *I can't believe Mrs. Brown is using that same excuse*, she thought. *She couldn't attend PTA or parent-teacher conference for the same reason. Some parents just try to get out of their responsibilities.*

Annie Lee edged close to the teacher's desk and the music box. Her eyes sparkled as she spoke and one finger tenderly traced the Madonna and child painted on the lid. "When my mother gets well, she's going to buy me a music box exactly like yours, Mrs. Stone."

The teacher smiled and answered, "That's nice, Annie Lee, but it couldn't be *exactly* like mine. You see, this is very old. It was my great-grandmother's music box. Someday, I'll give it to one of my children."

The following day Annie Lee brought a thin strip of red velvet ribbon to the teacher's desk.

"Mother went to the hospital last night but she gave me this ribbon to wrap around the gift I made for her," she said.

"The ribbon is very pretty," said Mrs. Stone. Then she added, "I'm sorry your mother is in the hospital."

"Daddy said I could bring the calendar to the hospital if you—"

Annie Lee began her request again, but Mrs. Stone interrupted. "I've already told you that we will wrap them tomorrow and take them home on Friday."

Annie Lee looked disappointed. Her face brightened, however, when she remembered the gift she had for her teacher. "Mother made this for you!" she said happily and laid a red velvet bookmark in front of Mrs. Stone. Then she turned and skipped away. The teacher noticed that the sheen was missing from the little girl's hair that day; it was dull and tangled and uncombed.

Friday came. The Christmas tree, somewhat over-decorated, stood in the center of the room. Mrs. Stone wore the cranberry red dress she wore every Christmas and Valentine's Day. The children entered the room noisily, each aware that Christmas was near. But Annie Lee's chair was empty.

Feeling uneasy, Mrs. Stone sat down. She did not want to know the reason Annie Lee was not at school: one more burden added to twenty-five years of accumulated frustrations was more than she could bear.

As if in answer to her unspoken question, a student monitor entered the room and handed her a folded note. Trembling, she read the principal's hastily written note: "I thought you'd want to know. Annie Lee Brown's mother died early this morning."

Somehow Mrs. Stone managed to get through the day. When the party was over and the children had gone home to enjoy their holiday, Mrs. Stone stood alone in her classroom and cried. She cried for Annie Lee, for Annie Lee's mother, and for herself—and for the calendar that was intended to bring joy but didn't, and the red velvet bookmark so undeserved.

Mrs. Stone left the school very late that night. Stars twinkled in the sky above, lighting the way to Annie Lee's house. In her hands, Mrs. Stone carried the precious music box as if it were the Wisemen's treasure itself. She looked up at the brightest star and prayed the music box would help return Christmas to both their hearts.

365 HOURS

The greatest gift I ever received was a gift I got one Christmas when my dad gave me a small box. Inside was a note saying, "Son, this next year I will give you 365 hours, an hour every day after dinner."

My dad not only kept his promise, but every year he renewed it and it's the greatest gift I ever had in my life.

Author unknown

The Storm

Tony Campolo
from 20 Hot Potatoes Christians Are Afraid to Touch

A friend of mine has an adorable four-year-old daughter. She is bright, and she is talkative. If tryouts were being held for a modern-day Shirley Temple, I think she would win, hands down.

One night there was a violent thunderstorm. The lightning flashed and the thunder rumbled—it was one of those terrifying storms that forces everyone to stop and tremble a bit. My friend ran upstairs to his daughter's bedroom to see if she were frightened and to assure her that everything would be all right. He got to her room and found her standing on the window sill, spread-eagled against the glass. When he shouted, "What are you doing?" she turned away from the flashing lightning and happily retorted, "I think God is trying to take my picture."

Family Picture

Gary Rosberg
from Guard Your Heart

I was sitting in my favorite chair, studying for the final stages of my doctoral degree, when Sarah announced herself in my presence with a question: "Daddy, do you want to see my family picture?"

"Sarah, Daddy's busy. Come back in a little while, Honey."

Good move, right? I *was* busy. A week's worth of work to squeeze into a weekend. You've been there.

Ten minutes later she swept back into the living room. "Daddy, let me show you my picture."

The heat went up around my collar. "Sarah, I said come back *later*. This is important."

Three minutes later she stormed into the living room, got three inches from my nose, and barked with all the power a five-year-old could muster: "Do you want to see it or don't you?" The assertive Christian woman in training.

"No," I told her, "I don't."

With that she zoomed out of the room and left me alone. And somehow, being alone at that moment wasn't as satisfying as I thought it would be. I felt like a jerk. (Don't agree so loudly.) I went to the front door.

"Sarah," I called, "could you come back inside a minute, please? Daddy would like to see your picture."

She obliged with no recriminations and popped up on my lap.

It was a great picture. She'd even given it a title. Across the top, in her best printing, she had inscribed: "OUR FAMILY BEST."

"Tell me about it," I said.

"Here is Mommy [a stick figure with long yellow curly hair], here is me standing by Mommy [with a smiley face], here is our dog Katie, and here is Missy [her little sister was a stick figure lying in the street in front of the house, about three times bigger than anyone else]. It was a pretty good insight into how she saw our family.

"I love your picture, Honey," I told her. "I'll hang it on the dining room wall, and each night when I come home from work and from class [which was usually around 10 PM], I'm going to look at it.

She took me at my word, beamed ear to ear, and went outside to play. I went back to my books. But for some reason I kept reading the same paragraph over and over.

Something was making me uneasy.

Something about Sarah's picture.

Something was missing.

I went to the front door. "Sarah," I called, "could you come back inside a minute, please? I want to look at your picture again, Honey."

Sarah crawled back into my lap. I can close my eyes right now and see the way she looked. Cheeks rosy from playing outside. Pigtails. Strawberry Shortcake tennis shoes. A Cabbage Patch doll named Nellie tucked limply under her arm.

I asked my little girl a question, but I wasn't sure I wanted to hear the answer.

"Honey...there's Mommy, and Sarah, and Missy. Katie the dog is in the picture, and the sun, and the house, and squirrels, and birdies. But Sarah...*where is your Daddy?*"

"You're at the library," she said.

With that simple statement my little princess stopped time for me. Lifting her gently off my lap, I sent her back to play in the spring sunshine. I slumped back in my chair with a swirling head and blood pumping furiously through my heart. Even as I type these words into the computer, I can feel those sensations all over again. It was a frightening moment. The fog lifted from my preoccupied brain for a moment—and suddenly I could see. But what I saw scared me to death. It was like being in a ship and coming out of the fog in time to see a huge, sharp rock knifing through the surf just off the port bow.

Sarah's simple pronouncement—"You're at the library"— got my attention big time.

FIRST DAY OF SCHOOL

On the first day of a new school year, the teacher used to send home a letter to every parent. It read, "If you promise not to believe all that your child tells you about what goes on at school, then I promise not to believe all he tells me about what goes on at home."

Author unknown

Ho-Ho-Ho-Sanna

Susan Larson

As a new parent I was eager to share with my two-year-old son Luke the true meaning of Christmas. We had planned a birthday party for baby Jesus and we had Luke's Opa build a small nativity set complete with stable, cows, wise men, shepherds, Mary, Joseph, and baby Jesus for him to play with. I was striving to keep Jesus' birthday the center of our Christmas celebration.

In our home we also had a two-foot-high musical Santa that lit up and loudly wished you Merry Christmas each time you shook his hand. Being concerned that Santa may be negatively impacting our focus on Christ's birthday, I asked my son Luke what Santa says. Luke proudly replied, "Ho-Ho-Ho Hosanna, Ha-Ha-Ha Hallelujah, He-He-He He saved me, I've got the joy of the Lord!"

Final Season

Bob Welch
from A Father for All Seasons

T he other night, after the parents had all come to pick up their sons and I was picking up catcher's equipment, bats and, of course, one forgotten mitt, it dawned on me that this was it: the last season I would coach one of my sons' baseball teams.

Two sons. Twelve seasons. Hundreds of games. Maybe three decent umps. And thousands of memories, hidden in my mind like all those foul balls lost in the creek behind the Ascot Park backstop.

Sitting in the rickety bleachers that spring evening, every one had gone—I found myself lost in thought, mentally walking along the creek, finding those long-forgotten foul balls and listening to the stories they had to tell.

The time our left fielder got locked in a Dairy Queen bathroom during a postgame celebration. The time I handed a protective cup to our new catcher and he thought it was an oxygen mask. The time a T-baller cleanly fielded a grounder, picked it up and tossed it to his mom, who was sitting behind third base reading Gone With the Wind.

For something that became more than a decade-long family affair, it had begun casually enough. While watching one of my five-year-old son's T-ball games in 1985, a manager asked if I would coach second base.

"Uh, second base?"

"Yeah. At this level you need coaches at second base or the kids will forget to take a left and wind up at Safeway."

So I coached second base. And before long, our family's summers revolved around a diamond: me coaching, my wife Sally keeping score, and the boys playing. Like the Israelites trudging out of Egypt, we hauled our equipment, lawn chairs, video cameras and sixty-four-ounce drinks from ballfield to ballfield, week after week, summer after summer.

The time our right fielder turned up missing during a championship game, only to be found at the snack bar eating licorice and flirting with girls. The time we showed up at an empty field, only to discover that I'd read the schedule wrong and our game was actually ten miles away.

The time I explained to my fifth-grade team that, because we'd given up eighty-nine runs in the last four games, we needed to set a defensive goal.

"It's a six-inning game," I explained. "Let's just try to hold them to twelve runs per game. Two per inning. Can you do that?"

Silence. Then my philosophical right fielder spoke up.

"Coach," he said, "do we have to give up the runs even like that, or could we like give up all twelve in the last inning?"

Our teams were more than a collection of kids. They were extended family, some of whom would end up sleeping overnight and going to church with us. And some of the boys desperately needed that. One year, of fifteen players, only five had a mother and father living together under the same roof. Once, a boy missed practice because his aunt had been murdered. And I can't count the number of times I took kids home because nobody came to pick them up.

But I've always remembered the advice I heard at a coaching clinic: "Who knows? The six hours a week you spend with a kid might be the only six hours that he actually feels loved."

The out-of-control coach who pushed me off the field. The kid who didn't get picked for my team firing a splat gun at our left fielder. The father who dropped off his son, Willie, and told him to get his own ride home; he and his girlfriend were going to a tavern to throw darts. We went into extra innings that afternoon, and the man's son played the game of his life, going all nine innings at catcher and making the game-winning hit.

We tried to make it more than just baseball. With help from our sons, we established a team newspaper. A few times I'd put candy in the sack at second base and let players dig in every time they threw out a runner. (Best defensive practice we ever had.)

Sally was our DH—designated healer—with her ever-present cooler of pop and packages of frozen corn for sprained ankles and bruised arms. Once, we had pizza delivered to the ballfield just after we'd lost to a team with one of those scream-and-yell coaches. I think we had more fun that night than the team that won.

The time we won with only eight players. The time Michael, a friend of my youngest son, spent the night at our house and played hours of backyard baseball, the rules stipulating that you must run the bases backward. The next morning, in a regulation game, Michael hit a hot grounder and promptly took off—for third base.

Over the years we won games, we lost games, and we lost baseballs—zillions of them. But for every ball we lost, we gained a memory. As a family, we laughed together, cried together, got dusty together—as if each of those hundreds of games was a microcosm of real life, which it was.

A weak-hitting kid named Cody stroking a three-run double and later telling his mom, "I'm trying to stop smiling, but I just can't."

My oldest son becoming my assistant coach and reaching a few kids in a way that I could not.

Kids I coached as third-graders now taller than I am.

And, of course, the night we were going to win the city championship. But for the first time in two months, it rained. Instead of playing on a field of dreams with perfectly straight white lines and a public address system, some official handed us a bunch of medals and called us cochamps.

Later that night, after the postseason pizza banquet, the restaurant manager approached me, broom in hand. "Excuse me, but are you the coach of the Washington Braves?"

"I sure am," I said, figuring he was going to pull me out of my doldrums by congratulating me on the cochampionship.

"Coach," he said, handing me the broom, "your team trashed the indoor play room. Wanna help sweep?"

Two sons. Twelve seasons. Hundreds of games. As a family, we had shared them all. But what, I wondered, had we missed in the process? What had we given up in order to pursue what some might see as trivia?

Nothing. Because whether your family is together at baseball games or camping trips or rodeos or dog shows or soccer tournaments or swim meets, the common denominator is this: families together—a rarity in our busy times—making memories. Learning lessons. Sowing seeds that can be nourished only by time.

Regrets? Only one. I wish Willie's father had considered his son more important than a game of darts. He missed seeing his teammates mob him after making the game-winning hit.

The time a tall third baseman was making fun of my 4-foot-9

*son at the plate—until my son nearly took off his head with a
line-drive double.*

My oldest son proudly posing for pictures with his grandparents after the team won a city championship.

*The time he played his final game and walking to the car
afterward, it hit me like a line drive in the side of the head. This
was it. I'd never coach him in baseball again.*

Dusk was descending. It was time to head for home where
my family—the boys were now seventeen and fifteen—would
be. As I slung the equipment bag over my shoulder and walked
down from the stands, I noticed a young father and his son
playing catch between short and third.

I smiled slightly and headed for the car, leaving behind
plenty of lost balls for others to find.

Love

IF I MARRY

If I marry: He must be so tall that when he is on his knees, he reaches all the way to heaven. His shoulders must be broad enough to bear the burden of a family. His lips must be strong enough to smile, firm enough to say no, and tender enough to kiss. He must be big enough to be gentle and great enough to be thoughtful. His arms must be strong enough to carry a little child

Ruth Bell Graham
from Ruth, A Portrait

Middle Man

Patsy Clairmont
from Normal Is Just a Setting on Your Dryer

ecause of a delay in taking off, my homebound flight was late, leaving me at risk of missing my second plane. When we landed at the connecting airport, I rushed through the terminal, arriving at my gate just as they were closing the doors. Relieved I'd made it, I headed down the aisle in search of my seat. I stopped at my assigned row and, to my dismay, found I had the middle seat.

There are some things I don't do. Middle seats head my "no way, I ain't gonna!" list. My mood swing went from "I'm so grateful I caught my plane" to "I don't care what this ticket says, I'm not sitting in that center seat!"

I glanced around and realized, however, that this was the last available seat on the flight, and I would sit there or on the wing. I prayed for an attitude adjustment. I remembered that God will operate on our attitudes but that He requires us to cooperate.

To do my part, I tried to think of a way to make this irritating situation fun. Then it came to me that I could pretend I was Oprah Winfrey and my seat partners were my guests. I would interview them. Now, this had possibilities!

I turned my interview efforts toward the man sitting next to me. I had already observed something about this young man when I was being seated. He called me "Ma'am." At the time I thought, *he must be in the service,* so I asked, "You in the service?"

"Yes, Ma'am, I am. The Marines."

"Hey, Marine, where are you coming from?"

"The Desert Storm, Ma'am."

"No kidding? How long were you there?" I continued.

"A year and a half. I'm on my way home. My family will

be at the airport. I'm so scared." As he said this last, he took in a short, nervous breath.

"Scared? Of what?" I asked.

"Oh, all this hero stuff. I'm not a hero, I'm just me, and I don't want my family to be disappointed."

"Take it from me, Marine, your parents just want you to come home safe."

Then Michael told me that when he lived at home, he and his mother were friends. When he joined the service and was stationed in Hawaii, they had written to each other and had become good friends. But when he went to Desert Storm, they became best friends.

"She will never know how she affected my life while I was away," he continued. "I've never thought of myself as a religious person, but while I was in the Storm, I learned to pray. The example I followed was the one my mom set for me when I was growing up."

"What was the most difficult time for you?" I inquired in Oprah fashion.

"There was a four-month space when we had not seen a woman or a child. The day we drove into Kuwait was very emotional for us. The women stood in doorways, waving, but even more moving was when the children ran to greet us. Since I've been stateside waiting to go home, I've been thinking about my nephews, and I can hardly wait to hear them call me Uncle Michael. The title *uncle* means even more to me than being called *sergeant*."

About that time, the flight attendant was passing by, and I tugged at her skirt. She looked down, and I said, "Know what? He is returning from Desert Storm."

The attendant asked him several questions and then requested that he write his name on a piece of paper. Taking his signature, she headed toward the front of the plane.

Moments later, the pilot came on the intercom and said, "It

has been brought to my attention that we have a VIP aboard. He is a returning GI from Desert Storm and is in seat 12F. As a representative of this airline and citizen of the United States of America, I salute you, Michael, and thank you for a job well done."

At that point, the entire plane burst into applause.

The pilot came back on and said, "We are making our final approach into the Detroit Metro Airport."

Michael's breath caught.

I looked up and saw his eyes had filled with tears. He peeked through a tear to see if I had noticed, and of course there I was, goggling at him.

He said softly, "I just don't want to cry."

"It's okay," I told him. "I checked a Marine manual on this one, and it's all right to cry. Some of the most admirable men I've ever known have shed tears at appropriate times, and Michael, this is a right time."

"Then you don't think I need to blame this on my contacts," he responded, grinning.

"I don't think so," I said with a giggle.

As our plane taxied in, I told him the best gift my son brought me when he returned from eighteen months in Guam was that after he made his way through the waiting crowd, he scooped me up in his arms and held me for a very long time.

It was time to deplane, and when Michael stood, the men all around us slapped him on the back and pumped his arm, thanking him for his contribution.

Michael's homecoming included a lineup of relatives armed with video equipment, flags, cameras, and banners. When we were close enough for eyes to focus in and distinguish which one was Michael, his family began to chant, "Michael, Michael, Michael."

Even from a distance, I could identify his mom. She was the one leaping the highest in the air. A guard leaned against the wall, watching to make sure no one stepped over the security line. But every time Michael's mom jumped into the air, she came down with her toe just over the line to let the guard know who was really in charge.

As we got closer, she stopped jumping, and her hands went over her mouth to muffle the building sobs. Tears poured down her arms and dropped off her elbows...just over the line.

I gave him a final nudge toward his family, and they engulfed him, everyone in tears. I saw Michael find his mom in the crowd and pull her into his arms and hold her for a very long time.

When we got to the baggage claim area, I prayed for the first time ever that my luggage would be delayed. Before long, the whole Desert Storm entourage came down to claim Michael's duffel bags.

Michael was still surrounded by family when I saw a youngster toddle over and pull on his pant leg. I realized this must be one of the nephews he was so eager to see again. When I noticed how young the boy was and remembered that Michael had been gone for a year and a half, I held my breath to watch how the boy would react to his uncle.

Michael's face lit up as he reached down and picked up the young boy. His nephew wrapped his chubby legs around the sergeant's waist, and his arms encircled Michael's neck. Then the boy's mom came over, and I heard her ask, "Honey, who's got you?"

He looked up, his young eyes reflecting his hero, and said, "Uncle Michael."

I could breathe again.

A few minutes later, the thought hit me that I almost missed being a part of this tender event because I hadn't wanted to sit in the middle.

Her Path of Love

Clare DeLong

L ooking out through our kitchen window we can see a path from our porch through the grass to the property adjoining ours. That property belongs to my mother— that path also belongs to her.

Some time ago, I was involved in a near fatal car accident. With nine bones broken and other injuries, I needed constant care and my future recovery meant a possible stay in a rehabilitation center.

My husband decided a few days before my discharge to take me home. The doctor approved and the equipment that would be needed was shipped and set up in the spare bedroom. Wally and Mom had accepted the responsibility of caring for me twenty-four hours a day.

That's when her path began. It continued to be used every day. For the next two and a half months Mom traveled that path in sunshine, rain, snow, and sleet, during the morning and afternoon hours, even sometimes in the middle of the night.

I call it her path of love. The things she did for me at that time are as many as the stars in the sky. She cared for me as only a mother could. Her love, tenderness, and gentleness shown to me will never be forgotten. Eighteen months later the path remains—a visible sign of a mother's love.

I'm Daddy's Girl

Becky Freeman
from Marriage 911

One evening not long ago, my husband stayed home with the children while I went to the grocery store. Shopping for a family of six when four of them are males takes a while, so it was late when I got home. When I walked back into the house, all was dark and unusually quiet. After setting down a bag of groceries, I tiptoed into the bedroom, lighted by the soft glow of the moon sifting through the window. Scott was lying there, his hands folded behind his head, staring at the ceiling. He seemed so pensive I immediately thought something was bothering him.

"Hey," I said softly and sat down on the bed beside him. "What's the matter?"

"Aw, I was just thinking about my daughter," he grinned sheepishly. "And how much I love her."

Evidently it had been a very good evening. "What happened with Rachel tonight?" I asked.

"Well," he sighed and searched for words to convey what he was feeling. "I had built a fire outside to burn some excess wood, and the telephone rang. It turned out to be a tough discussion with someone and I was upset. So I went outside to unwind by the fire, and, before long, our little girl came out of the house and snuggled by my side.

"'Dad,' she told me, 'you look like you could use a hug.'" He paused briefly and breathed a contented sigh.

"She's my little sweetheart, you know."

"I know," I smiled as I rubbed the back of my husband's neck. "And I hope she always will be."

The next evening Scott came home from work and found

me asleep on the couch. He woke me by tickling my nose with a long-stemmed red rose. Before I could properly gush over it, Rachel strolled in from her room, beaming from ear to ear. Her strawberry-blonde curls boing-yoinging happily as she plopped down on the sofa beside me. In her small, slender hands she held a lavender basket of fresh daisies and pink carnations. Tucked into the arrangement was a card in Scott's handwriting.

"Thanks for the hug," it read.

Rachel's brown eyes twinkled, and she smiled triumphantly in my direction. "You just got *one* flower. Daddy gave *me* a whole basket!"

NINE WORDS

Never forget the nine most important words of any family—
I love you.
You are beautiful.
Please forgive me.

H. Jackson Brown Jr.

50 Ways
to Love Your Children

Steve Stephens

1. Hug every morning.
2. Go to zoos, parades and amusement parks.
3. Hang their art and awards on the refrigerator.
4. Create family traditions.
5. Be patient.
6. Apologize when grumpy.
7. Go camping.
8. Play tic-tac-toe and hide n' seek.
9. Always carry Band-Aids and gumdrops.
10. Know their strengths.
11. Compliment them.
12. Encourage them.
13. Appreciate them.
14. Eat meals together.
15. Slow down.
16. Respect their privacy.
17. Listen.
18. Don't discipline in anger.
19. Be consistent.
20. Say "I love you" frequently.
21. Let them be silly.
22. Accept imperfections.
23. Reward good behavior.
24. Explain the rules clearly.
25. Laugh often.
26. Go to their favorite restaurant.
27. Invite their friends over.
28. Buy ice cream cones.

29. Go on vacations.
30. Know when to be gentle and when to be firm.
31. Make birthdays unforgettable.
32. Teach responsibility and respect.
33. Choose your battles.
34. Don't embarrass them.
35. Help with schoolwork.
36. Protect them.
37. Build memories.
38. Keep promises.
39. Say "no" when needed.
40. Don't yell.
41. Give gifts.
42. Model virtues.
43. Pray with them.
44. Pray for them.
45. Talk with their teachers.
46. Tell them you're proud of them.
47. Reach out.
48. Count stars together.
49. Talk every bedtime.
50. Let go with a blessing.

The Oak Tree

Max Lucado
from No Wonder They Call Him the Savior

I n a recent trip to my hometown I took some time to go see a tree. "A live oak tree," my dad had called it (with the accent on "live"). It was nothing more than a sapling, so thin I could wrap my hand around it and touch my middle finger to my thumb. The West Texas wind scattered the fall leaves and caused me to zip up my coat. There is nothing colder than a prairie wind, especially in a cemetery.

"A special tree," I said to myself, "with a special job." I looked around. The cemetery was lined with elms but no oaks. The ground was dotted with tombstones but no trees. Just this one. A special tree for a special man.

About three years ago Daddy began noticing a steady weakening of his muscles. It began in his hands. He then felt it in his calves. Next his arms thinned a bit.

He mentioned his condition to my brother-in-law, who is a physician. My brother-in-law, alarmed, sent him to a specialist. The specialist conducted a lengthy battery of tests—blood, neurological, and muscular—and he reached his conclusion. Lou Gehrig's disease. A devastating crippler. No one knows the cause or the cure. The only sure thing about it is its cruelty and accuracy.

I looked down at the plot of ground that would someday entomb my father. Daddy always wanted to be buried under an oak tree so he bought this one. "Special order from the valley," he had boasted. "Had to get special permission from the city council to put it here." (That wasn't hard in this dusty oil-field town where everybody knows everybody.)

The lump got tighter in my throat. A lesser man might

have been angry. Another man might have given up. But Daddy didn't. He knew that his days were numbered, so he began to get his house in order.

The tree was only one of the preparations he made. He improved the house for Mom by installing a sprinkler system and a garage door opener and by painting the trim. He got the will updated. He verified the insurance and retirement policies. He bought some stock to go toward his grandchildren's education. He planned his funeral. He bought cemetery plots for himself and Mom. He prepared his kids through words of assurance and letters of love. And last of all, he bought the tree. A live oak tree. (Pronounced with an accent on "live.")

Final acts. Final hours. Final words.

They reflect a life well lived.

The final hours are passing now. The gentle flame on his candle grows weaker and weaker. He lies in peace. His body dying, his spirit living. No longer can he get out of bed. He has chosen to live his last days at home. It won't be long. Death's windy draft will soon exhaust the flickering candle, and it will be over.

I looked one last time at the slender oak. I touched it as if it had been hearing my thoughts. "Grow," I whispered. "Grow strong. Stand tall. Yours is a valued treasure."

As I drove home through the ragged oil-field patchwork, I kept thinking about that tree. Though feeble, the decades will find it strong. Though slender, the years will add thickness and strength. Its last years will be its best. Just like my father's. Just like my Master's. "It is so much easier to die like Jesus if you have lived like him for a lifetime."

"Grow, young tree." My eyes were misting. "Stand strong. Yours is a valued treasure."

He was awake when I got home. I leaned over his bed. "I checked on the tree," I told him. "It's growing."

He smiled.

Head to Toe

Katherine G. Bond

Now that I'm four kids past twenty-five, my body shows some signs of wear and tear. So when we vacationed at a Washington coastal resort I was—I'll admit it—*jealous* of the flat-stomached, stretch-mark-free bachelorettes frolicking in the pool.

When the kids pulled out their swimsuits, I looked pleadingly at my husband, Andy. "Please take them in," I said. "I just can't go out in a swimsuit in front of all those twenty-somethings." He gave me a puzzled look, but took the children swimming while I watched the baby nearby.

That night Andy came in with a mysterious bag, from which he withdrew a bottle of...fuchsia nail polish!

"I'm going to paint your toenails," he announced.

"You're going to what?"

"Paint your toenails," he said, taking off my socks.

This is silly, I thought. *I don't even paint my toenails.*

But my husband was insistent.

"Why are you doing this?" I asked.

"Because," he answered, brushing on the first coat, "I want you to know you're beautiful from head to toe."

I looked at the guy who's been with me through fifteen years of bills and babies. He had not only protected me from embarrassment, but adorned me. I thought of those twenty-somethings with the flat stomachs and I didn't feel jealous anymore. Instead I felt grateful.

What to Give a Child

Billy Graham
from Billy Graham, The Inspirational Writings

A man and his wife visited an orphanage where they hoped to adopt a child. In an interview with the boy they wanted, they told him in glowing terms about the many things they could give him. To their amazement, the little fellow said, "If you have nothing to offer except a good home, clothes, toys, and the other things that most kids have—why—I would just as soon stay here."

"What on earth could you want besides those things?" the woman asked.

"I just want someone to love me," replied the little boy.

Season of the Empty Nest

Joan Mills
Reprinted with permission of
the Reader's Digest Association, Inc.

Remember when the children built blanket tents to sleep in? And then scrambled by moonlight to their own beds, where they'd be safe from bears? And how proud and eager they were to be starting kindergarten? But only up to the minute they got there? And the time they packed cardboard suitcases in such a huff? "You won't see *us* again!" they hollered. Then they turned back at the end of the yard because they'd forgotten to go to the bathroom?

It's the same thing when they're twenty or twenty-two, starting to make their own way in the grownup world. Bravado, pangs, false starts and pitfalls. They're half in, half out. "Good-bye, good-bye! Don't worry, Mom!" They're back the first weekend to borrow the paint roller and a fuse and a broom. Prowling the attic, they seize on the quilt the dog ate and the terrible old sofa cushions that smell like dead mice. "Just what I need!" they cheer, loading the car.

"Good-bye, good-bye!" implying forever. But they show up without notice at suppertimes, sighing soulfully to see the familiar laden plates. They go away again, further secured by four bags of groceries, the electric frying pan and a cookbook.

They call home collect, but not as often as parents need to hear. And their news makes fast-graying hair stand on end: "So he forgot to set the brake, and he says my car rolled three blocks backward down the hill before it was totaled!" "Simple case of last hired, first fired, no big deal. I sold the stereo, and..." "Mom! Everybody in the city has them! There's this roach stuff you put under the sink. It's..."

I gripped the phone with both hands in those days, wishing I could bribe my children back with everything they'd ever wanted—drum lessons, a junk-food charge account, anything. I struggled with an unbecoming urge to tell them once more about hot breakfasts and crossing streets and dry socks on wet days.

"I'm *so* impressed by how you cope!" I said instead.

The children scatter, and parents draw together, remembering sweet-shaped infants heavy in their arms, patched jeans, chicken pox, the night the accident happened, the rituals of Christmases and proms. With wistful pride and a feeling for the comic, they watch over their progeny from an effortfully kept distance. It is the season of the empty nest.

Slowly, slowly, there are changes. Something wonderful seems to hover then, faintly heard, glimpsed in illumined moments. Visiting the children, the parents are almost sure of it.

A son spreads a towel on the table and efficiently irons a perfect crease into his best pants. (*Ironing board*, his mother thinks, adding to a mental shopping list.) "I'm taking you to a French restaurant for dinner," the young man announces. "I've made reservations."

"Am I properly dressed?" his mother asks, suddenly shy. He walks her through city streets within the aura of his assurance. His arm lies lightly around her shoulders.

Or a daughter offers her honored guests the only two chairs she has and settles into a harem heap of floor pillows. She has raised plants from cuttings, framed a wall full of prints herself, spent three weekends refinishing the little dresser that glows in a square of sun.

Her parents regard her with astonished love. The room has been enchanted by her touch. "Everything's charming," they tell her honestly. "It's a real home."

Now? Is it *now*? Yes. The something wonderful descends. The generations smile at one another, as if exchanging congratulations.

The children are no longer children. The parents are awed to discover adults.

It *is* wonderful, in ways my imagination had not begun to dream on. How could I have guessed—how could they?—that of my three, the shy one would pluck a dazzling array of competencies out of the air and turn up, chatting with total poise, on TV shows? That the one who turned his adolescence into World War III would find his role in arduous, sensitive human service? Or that the unbookish, antic one, torment of his teachers, would evolve into a scholar, tolerating a student's poverty and writing into the night?

I hadn't suspected that my own young adults would be so ebulliently funny one minute, and so tellingly introspective the next; so open-hearted and unguarded. Or that growing up would inspire them to buy life insurance and three-piece suits and lend money to the siblings they'd once robbed of lollypops. Or that walking into their houses, I'd hear Mozart on the tape player and find books laid out for me to borrow.

Once, long ago, I waited nine months at a time to see who they would be, babes newly formed and wondrous. "Oh, *look!*" I said, and fell in love. Now my children are wondrously new to me in a different way. I am in love again.

My daughter and I freely share the complex world of our inner selves, and all the other worlds we know. Touched, I notice how her rhythms and gestures are reminding me of her grandmother's or mine. We are linked by unconscious mysteries and benignly watched by ghosts. I turn my head to gaze at her. She meets my look and smiles.

A son flies the width of the country for his one vacation in a whole long year. He follows me around the kitchen, tasting from the pots, handing down the dishes. We brown in the sun. Read books in silent synchrony. He jogs. I tend the flowers. We walk at the unfurled edge of great waves. We talk and talk, and later play cribbage past midnight. I'm utterly happy.

"But it's your vacation!" I remind him. "What shall we do that's special?"

"This," he says. "Exactly this."

When my children first ventured out and away, I felt they were in flight to outer space, following a curve of light and time to such unknowns that my heart would surely go faint with trying to follow. I thought this would be the end of parenting. Not what it is—the best part; the final, firmest bonding; the goal and the reward.

There's no vocabulary
for love within a family,
love that's lived in but not looked at,
love within the light of which all else is seen,
the love within which all other love finds speech.
This love is silent.

T. S. Eliot
from The Elder Statesman

Love's ABCs

Author unknown

Love
  Accepts, Behaves, Cheers, Defends,
  Enriches, Forgives, Grows and Helps.
Love
  Includes, Joins, Kneels, Listens,
  Motivates, Notices, Overlooks and
  Provides.
Love
  Quiets, Respects, Surprises, Tries,
  Understands, Volunteers, Warms,
  Xpects and Yields.
Love in action adds Zip to your life.

The Mystery of Marriage

Mike Mason
from The Mystery of Marriage

T he first thing I see, as I open my eyes, is the morning making a pink glow on the trunks of the three birch trees outside our window. Between two of the trunks hangs the moon, just past full and sinking in the west, the same pale, chalky-pink color as the papery bark of the birches. Both trees and moon appear almost translucent, as if lit from behind.

But the whole morning is translucent. The air holds light like a goblet. Even the mountain, that most opaque of God's creations, glows with an inner light…

This is the scene I wake up to every morning, here where I live, to the accompaniment of one of those frothing, silver-blue, rushing mountain rivers whose sound fills my ears the way the dawn light fills my eyes. And yet even that is not all. There is something else. Something more breathtaking than any of these other stupendous and beautiful things, and even more radiant with light.

There is a woman in bed beside me. Right this moment I could reach out my hand and touch her, as easily as I touch myself, and as I think about this, it is more staggering than any mountain or moon. It is even more staggering, I think, than if this woman happened instead to be an angel (which, come to think of it, she might well be). There are only two factors which prevent this situation from being so overpoweringly awesome that my heart would explode just trying to take it in: one is that I have woken up just like this, with the same woman beside me, hundreds of times before; and the other is that millions of other men and women are waking up beside each other, just like this, each and every day all around the world, and have been for thousands of years.

How do you divide your love among four children?
I don't divide it. I multiply it.

Bill Keene
from Family Circus

Her Hero

Paul Harvey
from Paul Harvey's For What It's Worth

I n the wake of Chicago's worst-ever winter, when all the rooftops were loaded (many overloaded) with snow, Robert McGrath saw his wife go into the backyard garage to fetch some boxes. Seconds later he heard the crash. Looking out, he saw the roof of the garage had caved in.

Without stopping for his hat or coat, McGrath ran from the house—grabbed a snow shovel—and called out for neighbors to help. Yelling and digging with his sweat freezing on his face, frantically throwing snow and pulling away boards, he heard her voice and then saw her hand!

He kept digging and throwing and pulling and within minutes he had his wife in his arms and was sobbing, "Are you all right?"

She was all right.

I would not tell you what I am about to tell except that a neighbor saw and snitched...

Mrs. McGrath had gone into the garage through one door and out through another. She was safe in the house when she looked out and saw her husband digging and shouting orders and throwing lumber and she couldn't let her gallant rescuer down. She put her coat on again and went back out and went back in through the back door of the garage and allowed husband Bob to be her hero.

A Time to Dance

Jane Kirkpatrick
from A Burden Shared

His broken ankles and hip, her shattered foot and arm left them helpless for a time, the airplane accident taking its toll. One day the casts came off and they thought they'd dance for joy, to ballroom music, in the city, the way they had before the clatter and crash of metal against pavement. But they couldn't. Too much pain, recovery not yet present though the bones looked stronger and the X-rays showed the breaks had mended. Deep healing takes more time.

A year passed. On a Saturday morning, wearing blue coveralls, he asked her to dance, there in the living room with the dogs lying surprised at the feet of their masters' strange movements. Gently, he began to swirl her about the room, his wide hands holding her close to feel the slight adjustments he should make. She accommodated for how his broken hip had healed; he compensated for her shattered foot and her now fused arch.

Their arms held differently, aware of each other's needs, they now could dance. They eased around the living room, smiles reflecting in each others' eyes while music played. A slight adjustment, accommodation and realignment and they danced on. Isn't that what life's about? Some fixing and fine tuning over time, aware of breaks and the patience needed for mending.

Roses

Author unknown

An old man got on a bus one February 14 carrying a dozen red roses. He sat beside a young man. The young man looked at the roses and said, "Somebody's going to get a beautiful Valentine's Day gift."

"Yes," said the old man.

A few minutes went by and the old man noticed that his young companion was staring at the roses. "Do you have a girl-friend?" the old man asked.

"I do," said the young man. "I'm going to see her now. I'm taking her this." He held up a Valentine's Day card.

They rode along in silence for another ten minutes, and the old man rose to get off the bus. As he stepped out into the aisle, he suddenly placed the roses on the young man's lap and said, "I think my wife would want you to have these. I'll tell her that I gave them to you."

He left the bus quickly, and as the bus pulled away, the young man turned to see the old man enter the gates of a cemetery.

Good Choice

Liz Curtis Higgs
from Reflecting His Image

F lying home from Atlanta one Saturday evening, I sat next to a young woman who was impeccably groomed in every way, except for the streaks on her cheeks where tears had removed some of her soft red blush.

My heart went out to her, but my head said, *None of your business, Liz. Don't interfere.*

As usual, I ignored my head and went with my heart. "What brings you to Louisville?" I asked softly.

She turned in my direction, and a fresh flow of tears began as she moaned, "I don't know!"

Inside, a still, small voice said, *Hush...let her talk!* So I pressed my lips together (for me, that's almost an aerobic exercise), assumed my most compassionate expression, and nodded.

"I'm g-g-getting married," she stammered, daintily blowing her perfectly powdered nose.

"How wonderful!" I exclaimed, despite my vow of silence.

"I'm not so sure," she said, her voice still shaking. "My entire family and all my friends live in Florida, plus I have a great job there. I'm leaving my whole life behind." Another trickle of tears slipped out of the corner of her eye.

"I moved to Louisville from far away too," I said, trying to encourage her. "It's a great place to live."

"I guess so," she said, sounding unconvinced.

Despite my efforts, I was not helping one bit. Then, the perfect question suddenly presented itself: "Do you love him?"

Her expression changed instantly. "Oh, yes!" she said, then blushed at her own enthusiasm. "He's very kind and considerate, really intelligent, and handsome, too." As she brushed away the last of her tears, she told me all about her beloved fiancé, how much fun they had together, how impressed her family was with him, and yes, how much she loved him. I smiled, nodded, and listened, knowing no further questions would be needed.

When we landed and headed into the gate area, I picked him out of the crowd instantly. Even from a distance, he was obviously a fine young man. Tall, strong, yet with a warm and gentle smile and armed with a dozen red roses that matched her red suit perfectly. When she ran into his arms with a teary smile, I made myself look away (very difficult!) rather than invade their privacy but found a few happy tears had sneaked into my own eyes.

HOW TO MAKE LOVE ENDURE

Be a good kisser.
It might make your wife forget
that you never take out the trash.

Randy, age 8

A Signal at Night

Charlotte Adelsperger

T he local hospital had become my new, temporary home as our eighteen-month-old son, John, struggled with a respiratory infection. At first John's rapid breathing and ballooning chest had caused me to tremble in fear. But after a few days of aggressive medical treatment and many prayers, John began to improve.

Even though I was thanking God with my whole heart, I was exhausted from trying to sleep on a reclining chair in John's hospital room. I missed our little three-year-old, Karen, and my husband Bob.

One particular evening Bob came to be with John and me. We chatted about John's improved condition, and how Karen was getting along at home.

All too soon Bob glanced at his watch. "Visiting hours are over; I really have to go," he said. He hugged me; then kissed me gently.

"I don't want you to leave," I said, my eyes filling with tears. "But I know you must." How I wished I could just be with my whole family again!

Bob gave me another hug. "Look down there," he said, pointing through the window to where his car was parked. "I'll be driving right past your room. Stand here at the window. When I come by, I'll blink my lights. It'll be my little signal that I love you, and I'll be thinking of you.

Minutes later I recognized our car as it slowly moved on the street below. The lights blinked on, then off. A few more feet and another blink, and then another. As it turned onto the main street, another. The lights kept blinking until my blurred eyes could no longer see them. Then I noticed the stars of God's heavens. They were blinking too—*I love you. I love you.* And I thought, *Isn't that the signal God wants for all of his children every night?*

How much the wife is dearer than the bride.

George, Lord Lyttleton

Little Red Boots

Jeannie Williams

My granddaughter Tate turned five years old recently, and her mother gave her a very special present: a pair of red cowgirl boots that had been her own when she was a little girl. Tate pulled on the little red boots and began to dance around the room. It is always fun to dress up in Mom's clothes when you are a little girl, but when Mom's clothes are your own size, well, the excitement is almost uncontainable.

Kelly, my daughter-in-law, told us about the first time she wore her boots. You see, not only did she experience the thrill of wearing her first pair of real cowgirl boots, she also experienced the thrill of meeting her first love.

He was an older man: she was five and he was seven. He lived in the city and his father brought him to Kelly's grandfather's farm one Saturday afternoon to ride the horses. Kelly sat on the top fence rail as Grandfather saddled her pony. She was trying very hard not to get her shiny new red boots dirty when the city boy came over to say hello. He smiled at her and admired her new boots. It must have been love at first sight because Kelly offered to let him ride her pony. She had never let *anyone* ride her pony before.

Later that year, Grandfather sold the farm and Kelly didn't see the young man again. But Kelly never forgot that magical moment in her childhood, and she thought of the city boy every time she put on her red cowgirl boots. When she outgrew them, her mother packed them away. Years later, while organizing for a garage sale, Kelly found the little red boots and decided to give them to Tate for her birthday.

Tate's laughter brought us back to the present. My son, Marty, scooped his giggling daughter into his arms and danced around the room with her. "I do like your new cowgirl boots, baby," he said. "They remind me of the day I rode my very first pony. I wasn't much older than you are."

"Is this a true story, Daddy? Or a make-believe one?" Tate loved to listen to her daddy tell stories about when he was a little boy. "Does it have a happy ending?" Then she begged him to tell her about his first pony ride. Marty smiled at Tate's unending string of questions as he sat down in the big, comfortable recliner. Tate climbed up into his lap.

"Once upon a time when I was seven years old I lived in the big city called St. Louis. That's in Missouri. I wanted a horse more than anything in the world, but we couldn't have one in the city. I told my dad that I wanted to be a real cowboy when I grew up, so that summer he took me to a farm not very far from here. And I got to ride a real pony for the very first time."

You can guess how Marty's story ends, but as incredible as it sounds, Marty and Kelly had no idea they had met as children until the day of their daughter's fifth birthday. What's more, the little boy from the city did grow up to be a real cowboy: Marty's now a team roper in professional rodeos.

True stories have happy endings, too!

People who really love each other are the happiest people in the world... They love their children and they love their families. They may have very little...but they are happy.

Mother Teresa
from No Greater Love

Memories

REUNION

We all gather once again—young and old, introvert and life-of-the-party, freckled cousins and smiling grandmothers, whose eyes brim with pride and happy memories. What would the day be without brothers, dads and sons sharing the latest jokes and achievements. It is a time for the family to reaffirm itself and grow. To bond with newlyweds and precious little ones lost. It's a day to laugh and hug and remember who we are.

Donna Green
from To My Daughter, with Love

Stories on a Headboard

Elaine Pondant
Reprinted with permission from the
March 1994 Reader's Digest

The bed was about 45 years old when Mom passed it along to me a few months after my father died. I decided to strip the wood and finish it for my daughter Melanie. The headboard was full of scratches.

Just before starting to take the paint off, I noticed that one of the scratches was a date: September 18, 1946, the day my parents were married. Then it struck me—this was the first bed they had as husband and wife!

Right above their wedding date was another name and date: "Elizabeth, October 22, 1947."

My mother answered the phone. "Who is Elizabeth," I asked, "and what does October 22, 1947, mean?"

"She's your sister."

I knew Mom had lost a baby, but I never saw this as anything more than a misfortune for my parents. After all, they went on to have five more children.

"You gave her a name?" I asked.

"Yes. Elizabeth has been watching us from heaven for 45 years. She's as much a part of me as any of you."

"Mom, there are a lot of dates and names I don't recognize on the headboard."

"June 8, 1959?" Mom asked.

"Yes. It says 'Sam.'"

"Sam was a black man who worked for your father at the plant. Your father was fair with everyone, treating those under him with equal respect, no matter what their race or religion. But there was a lot of racial tension at that time. There was also a union strike and a lot of trouble.

"One night some strikers surrounded your dad before he got to his car. Sam showed up with several friends, and the crowd dispersed. No one was hurt. The strike eventually ended, but your dad never forgot Sam. He said Sam was an answer to his prayer."

"Mom, there are other dates on the headboard. May I come over and talk to you about them?" I sensed the headboard was full of stories. I couldn't just strip and sand them away.

Over lunch, Mom told me about January 14, 1951, the day she lost her purse at a department store. Three days later, the purse arrived in the mail. A letter from a woman named Amy said: "I took five dollars from your wallet to mail the purse to you. I hope you will understand." There was no return address, so Mom couldn't thank her, and there was nothing missing except the five dollars.

Then there was George. On December 15, 1967, George shot a rattlesnake poised to strike my brother Dominick. On September 18, 1971, my parents celebrated their silver wedding anniversary and renewed their vows.

I learned about a nurse named Janet who stayed by my mother and prayed with her after my sister Patricia's near-fatal fall from a swing. There was a stranger who broke up the attempted mugging of my father but left without giving his name.

"Who is Ralph?" I asked.

"On February 18, 1966, Ralph saved your brother's life in Da Nang. Ralph was killed two years later on his second tour of duty."

My brother never spoke about the Vietnam War. The memories were deeply buried. My nephew's name is Ralph. Now I knew why.

"I almost stripped away these remarkable stories," I said. "How could you give this headboard to me?"

"Your dad and I carved our first date on the headboard the

night we married. From then on, it was a diary of our life together. When Dad died, our life together was over. But the memories never die."

When I told my husband about the headboard, he said, "There's room for a lot more stories."

We moved the bed with the story-book headboard into our room. My husband and I have already carved in three dates and names: Barbara and Greg and Jackson. Someday, we'll tell Melanie the stories from her grandparents' lives. And someday the bed will pass on to her.

DAD

He dreams, he plans,
he struggles that we might have the best.
His sacrifice is quiet, his life is love expressed.

Author unknown

Enjoy the Ride!

Barbara Johnson
from Joy Breaks

Yesterday is a sacred room in your heart where you keep your memories. Here you cherish laughter from another day. You hear melodies of half-forgotten songs. You feel the warmth of a hug from an old friend. You see the lingering glow of a long-gone love. From your yesterdays you draw lessons and encouragement to pass along to others.

My heart smiled at some yesterdays recently when I thought back on teaching my oldest son, Tim, how to drive. We practiced in a nearby cemetery where it was quiet, the posted speed limits were very slow, and traffic was sparse. *A nice, safe place to start*, I thought.

Tim would work his way around the curves and turns, carefully maneuvering the car through its paces. Brake into the curve. Gently. Accelerate out of the curve. Slowly. Smoothly. Stop. Reverse. Back up. Park between the lines. Try it again. Start all over again.

Afterward, we'd go over to In-N-Out Hamburgers across the street where I would recover from the experience. After we ate, Tim would want to tackle the curves again. Sometimes I wondered if I would survive until he actually learned how to drive.

Well, I did. Tim did learn. And he was a good driver. But years later, his car was smashed by someone who wasn't. Now, Tim's grave is right up there where he practiced driving.

I could be bitter about it. Or I can be better. When yesterdays bring bittersweet memories, I can fume and blame my losses on someone else, or I can let my memories comfort me and provide encouragement to someone else.

As I was standing by Tim's grave recently and thinking of the many times we wound around those curving lanes, I remembered how I used to feel: nervous and tense but trying not to show it. My reverie by Tim's headstone was interrupted when a little red Nissan came around the curve. There was a mother, about thirty-five, her hair blowing in the breeze. Beside her, in the driver's seat, sat a boy, about fifteen, cute as anything. The mom's face looked intent while the boy tried to look nonchalant.

I wanted to shout out, "Enjoy the ride! Now! Make a memory of your experience. Go get a hamburger to celebrate. Do it now, while you still can look each other in the eyes!"

Yes, it hurts. I wish Tim were here, driving me to some of the places I need to go occasionally, just for old times' sake. I long for the family circle—unbroken—the way it will be in heaven. I want to hear my boy's laughter again and the way he used to rush in the house and call, "Mom!" I envy that mom in the little red Nissan, but I know the years end up stealing something from everybody. And I just want to tell that woman to savor the moment. Taste the present full strength. Do everything you can to hold it close.

This week when I go do the things I have to do, I'll take my own advice. I'll look people in the eyes, and if they don't have a smile, I'll give them one of mine. I'll make a date with my husband or play a joke on a friend. I won't let time pass without reminding myself, "Enjoy the ride!"

The Nest

Evelyn Petty

Our front door slammed open and shut many times over the years, but there was one summer it was silenced— the summer before the last of our three children left for college. Christine, John and Jeff had been fun to raise and the delight of my life. Even the thought of them leaving home felt empty.

One day, I noticed a mother bird feverishly making a nest on the light fixture by our front door. Twigs and debris were scattered on the ground underneath. Somewhat anxious brown eyes peered quietly over the edge at me.

From that time forward, the front door was off limits. Through the entire active summer, with two kids home from college and another one preparing to leave, everyone used the kitchen door. Soon, the nest burst into activity with the arrival of three little birds. We were able to watch from the kitchen as the mother bird fed and fluffed her babies, cleaned out the nest and eventually taught them to fly. And then one day, they were gone.

I thought about the mother bird and how her care and tending had ended as the birds flew away leaving nothing but a nest. From the moment I counted the three birds, I began identifying with the whole process, so I carefully took the abandoned home down from its perch and placed it on a shelf in the garage. As I watched Chris, and John, and now Jeff pack to leave home, I wept realizing the inevitable had come; I had raised my family and it was time for them to apply all the lessons home had taught them.

Late in October of the same year, an unusually loud thunderstorm hit our area. I looked out the kitchen window at the sky and a movement caught my eye. There, huddled under the eaves by the front door, near the porch light, were three fledgling birds. I'm sure it was "our family," returning to find shelter in the only place they knew for sure was safe, familiar, welcoming—because it was home.

Smiling, I returned to my breakfast, knowing I'd been given reassurance. Though the years of nurturing were over, the years ahead would bring many opportunities for sheltering our family. When the crisis, the frightening, the difficult or the overwhelming times come, there is one place that will always be safe, familiar, welcoming for my family—home.

Home to laughter, home to rest,
Home to those we love the best...
Now the day is done and I
Turn to hear a welcoming cry.
Love is dancing at the door,
I am safe at home once more.

Author unknown

The Reading Chair

Faith Andrews Bedford

I t is a warm, sunshiny afternoon. As I read by the window, the sounds of children playing outside spark memories of long-ago summer days. For a moment, I think I hear my mother's voice calling my name.

As Mother's voice comes closer, I quickly slip behind my father's big red leather chair. All afternoon I have been nestled in it, reading. Now I have only fifty pages more until I've finished *The Black Stallion*. I know that if Mother finds me, she will make me go outside to play. "What are you doing inside on such a beautiful day?" she will ask. Then she'll tell me to run outdoors and find the other children. So I hide.

Father's red leather chair occupied a corner of his study, a large room filled with floor-to-ceiling bookcases. Beside the chair stood an old library table whose worn top supported a jumble of books, magazines, papers, pens, crayons, and games—all gathered beneath a brass lamp with a leaded-glass shade. Beneath the table, we piled the library books my sisters and I brought home each week.

On the other side of the chair was a bookcase whose three bottom shelves were devoted to children's books. Some of these had been gifts to my parents; their musty pages and worn leather bindings testified to many readings. The inside cover of *Little Women* bore my grandmother's flowery script: "To Joan, Merry Christmas, 1932." Several volumes with wonderful illustrations, including *Treasure Island* and *Ivanhoe*, were inscribed "To Jimmy on his birthday. From Father." Mixed in with these were my books: *Anne of Green Gables*, *Misty of Chincoteague*, and the Bobbsey Twins' adventures, Nancy Drew mysteries, and fairy tales ranging from the Brothers

Grimm to Hans Christian Andersen.

During the day, when Father was at work, the red leather chair was my favorite place to be. I would curl up in it and read for hours, my legs dangling over its smooth arms. Since the chair was big enough to embrace two children, one of my little sisters would often join me in it, first choosing a book for me to read aloud and reminding me to "please do all the voices." Sometimes Mother squeezed into Father's chair with me. Scary stories were somehow better when Mother read them. When Father came home, though, the chair became his once more— and he filled it completely. After dinner, he would retire to his quiet corner, open his briefcase, delve into office work, and, later, fall asleep over the newspaper.

Each time our family moved into a new home, the chair moved with us, growing older and more worn ("more comfortable" said my father) with each journey. For a while, it stood in a corner of our basement playroom, and after I left for college, Mother bought Father a new, tweed-covered reading chair and put the old relic in the attic. I tried the dapper new chair out a few times; it wasn't the same.

When my husband and I bought our first home, we combed thrift shops, yard sales, and our families' attics and basements, looking for any cast-off furniture we might claim. Over by the window in my parents' attic, I spotted the red leather chair. I dusted it off, slid into it, reached over to a pile of old *National Geographic* magazines, and settled in for a good read. It felt like home and it was dusk before my husband found me. "You want that old thing?" he asked, eyeing the chair's scuffed legs and sagging seat.

The red leather chair has moved with my own family several times. My husband has discovered that it is a welcoming chair despite its age. The smooth, cool leather warms up after a few moments, and the supple cushions curve around each reader's special shape. Every year, on Father's birthday, I give his chair a good cleaning with saddle soap, rubbing it until the mellow leather glows like a ruby.

When my children were small, their books were always stacked beside the red chair, which was relegated by its faded elegance to the family room or a study. With a bit of wriggling, one mother and two children would fit in it for bedtime stories. There I read *Heidi* to my children as I had to my little sisters years earlier. I "did all the voices" for *Charlotte's Web* and wept all over again. When my children began to read, that was the chair they chose as their own. Curled up in it, they discovered the adventures of Laura and Mary Ingalls, the girls I met via the *Little House on the Prairie* books I carried home from my school's library so many years earlier.

Now, with my children grown and gone, I have returned to school. To ease the commute, I've taken a small apartment near the campus and have furnished the tiny space with a few old things: a bed, a table and chairs, a desk, and the red leather chair. It is my reading chair, although the books I'm reading lately are a far cry from *Black Beauty* and not nearly as much fun as fairy tales. No Nancy Drew book ever had footnotes, and there was no need to highlight Dr. Seuss.

Years of reading and learning have penetrated this chair. In it, three generations have been transported to other times and other places. We have been introduced to new ideas, theories, and points of view. When I sink into its cushions and settle down for a few hours' reading, I become quickly absorbed; the pages fly by and I, once again, lose track of time.

Now, as the evening light falls across my book and children's laughter fades in the distance, I recall the times when I would hide behind this old red chair, not daring to breathe until Mother's footsteps had receded. Returning to my studies, I am content knowing I may read as long as I like and no one is going to make me go play outside.

A New Hat for Shane

Rhonda Wehler

The toddler cowboy boots were scuffed on both toes and creased at the heels. I vowed to bronze them someday as I packed them into the steamer trunk along with a well-worn Piglet and a handmade baby quilt. How I wished I had kept Shane's beige, felt cowboy hat that had slouched over his forehead. My mind flooded with memories as I leaned against the wall and remembered my son's growing-up years.

Shane's fondness for hats grew as he did. I recalled him as a toddler wearing a hat and reading upside-down Dr. Seuss books while sitting in his small-scale rocker. Shane alternated between a chocolate-brown hobo hat, a red cowboy hat, and an oversized western hat that had long since lost its shape. Later, a multicolored beanie was added to Shane's collection after he learned his Bible verses for the "Good News Club."

In elementary school, Shane created his own head covering for a Christmas performance. His shepherd headgear was fashioned by tying an arm cover from the plaid couch around his forehead with twine. In the years that followed, he sported softball helmets, tennis visors, ball caps, "I Love Fishing" hats, camouflage hunting caps and hard hats.

As Shane's taste in hats developed, so did his desire to make his own way. Once at a fifth-grade track meet, we watched the typical Oregon partly sunny sky succumb to rain. Determined not to let the inclement weather dampen my son's enthusiasm, I edged close to the track. When the gun sounded for Shane's heat, I shouted with gusto, "Go, Bobbalou!"

As he crossed the finish line, I whooped and hollered and patted him on the back. Although he had run well, Shane had a sullen look on his face. "Mom," he sternly admonished, "don't ever call me Bobbalou in public again."

Several months later, Shane called me into his room one night for a talk. As I sat down on his bed, he counseled me, "Mom, I don't want to hurt your feelings, but please don't sing "All Aboard for Blanket Bay" to me at bedtime anymore. After all, I *am* in middle school now." Shane was growing up. I got that message loud and clear.

When the day arrived that I left him waving on the curb of a college two thousand miles from home, I felt as if part of me had been amputated. I realized that my son would acquire strength only if I allowed him to exercise his power of choice. But knowing that did nothing to alleviate my fear that his decisions might cause him pain. The days of holding him on my lap and whispering words of comfort were gone. Instead, I had to release this one I loved so much to the One who loved him more.

Shane eventually chose a wife. She was from the mountains of Montana where real-life cowboys still make their living. It was no surprise to me that on his wedding day Shane wore a black tux with tails—and a new, black Stetson. During the ceremony, Shane watched just inches from me as his bride approached on her father's arm. I wanted to reach out and squeeze his arm, but I resisted. I sensed this was a pivotal moment—a rite of passage for me as well as him.

As Shane confidently stepped forward and extended his arm to his bride, my heart constricted with emotions...pride and love for this precious son who was stepping into regions unknown with a new partner, and momentary sadness for our relationship which was from that moment altered forever.

As I watched Shane and his wife exchange their wedding vows, I consciously exchanged *my* role as his primary nurturer to that of their No. 1 encourager. I sensed that only as I completely released my son to move forward with his life would I be freed to fully enter into the thrill of watching him grow into manhood. Shane, indeed, wore a new hat that day. And so, I realized, did I.

I sighed as I locked the trunk and returned it to storage. Someday I really will bronze those boots. And even though the old felt cowboy hat never found a place in the keepsake chest, it will always be a priceless symbol to me of a lifetime of growth—for my son *and* myself.

She is clothed with strength and dignity;
she can laugh at the days to come...
Her children arise and call her blessed;
her husband also, and he praises her;
"Many women do noble things,
but you surpass them all."

Proverbs 31:25, 28–29

Highest Honor

Stu Weber
from Four Pillars of a Man's Heart

I am writing these words on a Monday. I've just come from delivering the message at a funeral for an old friend, a member of our local church...

Don's service today was a fitting tribute to a great man. In the foyer just outside the auditorium, his four grown daughters had created a display that did him proud. There was his beret and pictures from his days in the military, along with training certificates and military awards. Alongside this was memorabilia from his twenty-one years with the U.S. Forest Service after his time in the military. Also represented was the small construction company Don founded when he retired from the Forest Service. And there were family pictures, too. Great shots of smiling, confident people. His wife, his daughters, and their children.

But one item stole the show. Don would likely tell you it was probably the highest award (other than Shirley's "yes!" to his marriage proposal) he had ever received. It was a poem written shortly after he died, by one of his daughters, now a mother herself. As people filed by the display, each stopped to read that centerpiece. Virtually every one of them, both men and women, struggled to hold back their tears. Many didn't succeed. I didn't. Here is what we read:

Dad, are you really gone?
I'm certain I was there when you took your last breath.
Yet it seems your life is still speaking so loud and clear.

Are you really gone?
   I can see you in all my childhood days
   Always taking care of us, letting our lives as children
   Be as God intended: carefree, happy and adventurous,
   joyful.

Are you really gone?
   I can see your smile and your fatherly wink
   As I feel your familiar and vigorous hug.
   I can see the joy in your face as your grandchildren
   embrace you and you turn to me without hesitation
   And say, "You're a good mother, I'm proud of you."

Are you really gone?
   I can see you so clear, a man of God, a devoted father,
   A loving husband, a church leader, a friend,
   I can hear you say, "It's good to be alive,"
   As you enjoy the simple pleasures in life.

Are you really gone?
   I can see your Christian influence woven into the deci-
   sions of my life and it is only by your confident example
   that I can say,
   You'll never really be gone from us.
   And I can now hear our heavenly Father say to you,
   "Welcome, good and faithful servant,
   Enter into the joy I have prepared for you."

   It doesn't get any better than that. No medal, ribbon, or
citation even remotely compares to the deep, abiding love and
respect of a daughter or son.

The Bobby Pins

Linda Goodman

When I was seven years old, I overheard my mother tell one of her friends that the following day was to be her thirtieth birthday. Two things occurred to me when I heard that: one, I had never before realized that my mother had a birthday; and two, I could not recall her ever getting a birthday present.

Well, I could do something about that. I went into my bedroom, opened my piggy bank and took out all the money that was inside: five nickels. That represented five weeks' worth of my allowance. Then I walked to the little store around the corner from my house, and I told the proprietor, Mr. Sawyer, that I wanted to buy a birthday present for my mother.

He showed me everything in his store that could be had for a quarter. There were several ceramic figurines. My mother would have loved those, but she already had a house full of them and I was the one who had to dust them once a week. They definitely would not do. There were also some small boxes of candy. My mother was diabetic, so I knew they would not be appropriate.

The last thing Mr. Sawyer showed me was a package of bobby pins. My mother had beautiful long black hair, and twice a week she washed and pincurled it. When she took the pincurls down the next day, she looked just like a movie star with those long, dark curls cascading around her shoulders. So I decided those bobby pins would be the perfect gift for my mother. I gave Mr. Sawyer my five nickels, and he gave me the bobby pins.

I took the bobby pins home and wrapped them in a colorful sheet from the Sunday comics (there was no money left for wrapping paper). The next morning, I walked up to my mother and handed her that package and said, "Happy birthday, Momma!"

My mother sat there for a moment in stunned silence. Then, with tears in her eyes, she tore at that comic-strip wrapping. By the time she got to the bobby pins, she was sobbing.

"I'm sorry, Momma!" I apologized. "I didn't mean to make you cry. I just wanted you to have a happy birthday."

"Oh, honey, I am happy!" she told me. And I looked into her eyes, and I could see that she was smiling through her tears. "Why, do you know that this is the first birthday present that I have ever received in my entire life?" she exclaimed.

Then she kissed me on the cheek and said, "Thank you, honey." And she turned to my sister and said, "Lookee here! Linda got me a birthday present!" And she turned to my father and said, *"Lookee here! Linda got me a birthday present!"*

And then she went into the bathroom to wash her hair and pincurl it with her new bobby pins.

After she left the room, my father looked at me and said, "Linda, when I was growing up, back on the frontier (my daddy always called his childhood home in the mountains of Virginia *the frontier*), we didn't set much store by giving birthday presents to adults. That was something done just for small young 'uns. And your momma's family, they were so poor, they didn't even do that much. But seeing how happy you've made your momma today has made me rethink this whole birthday issue. What I'm trying to say, Linda, is I believe you have set a precedent here."

And I did set a precedent. After that, my mother was showered with birthday presents every year: from my sister, from my brothers, from my father and from me. And, of course, the older we children got, the more money we made, and the nicer presents she received. By the time I was twenty-five, I had given her a stereo, a color television and a microwave oven (which she traded in for a vacuum cleaner).

For my mother's fiftieth birthday, my brothers and my sister and I pooled our resources and got her something spectacular: a ring set with a pearl surrounded by a cluster of diamonds. And when my oldest brother handed that ring to her at the party that was given in her honor, she opened up the velvet gift box and peered at the ring inside. Then she smiled and turned the box around so that her guests could see her special gift, and she said, "Don't I have wonderful children?" Then she passed the ring around the room, and it was thrilling to hear the collective sigh that rippled through that room as the ring was passed from hand to hand.

After the guests were gone, I stayed to help clean up. I was doing the dishes in the kitchen when I overheard a conversation between my mother and father in the next room. "Well, Pauline," my father said, "that's a mighty pretty ring you've got there. I reckon that's about the best birthday present you've ever had."

My own eyes filled with tears when I heard her reply. "Ted," she said softly, "that's a might pretty ring and that's a fact. But the best birthday present I ever got? Well, that was a package of bobby pins."

A little girl, when asked where her home was, replied,
"Where Mother is."

Keith L. Brooks

The Map

Jane Ann Clark

Memories of Aunt Wanda crowded into my mind. Aunt Wanda in the kitchen, her ample form covered by a checked apron. The smell of banana bread drifting across the room as she said, "Keep your grubby fingers outta my cookie jar, you little cookie monster." The twinkle in her eyes softened the rebuke.

Aunt Wanda's rose garden. Who would tend her roses? They were used to Aunt Wanda's sweet voice and caressing touch as she coaxed them into bloom.

Community Church would never be the same without Aunt Wanda. She didn't have a beautiful singing voice, but somehow I knew God loved to hear her sing. When Wanda sang "Amazing Grace," tears of gratitude coursed down her weathered cheeks.

But what I remember most is the summer I was ten. I awoke at about two o'clock in the morning and heard a voice softly speaking. A dim light filtered into my room from down the hall.

I silently tiptoed through the darkness and peeped around the door into Aunt Wanda's antique-filled bedroom. She was sitting in the middle of her big four-poster bed with photographs scattered out in front of her and a big ol' map of the world lying beside her.

I watched from my hiding place as she lovingly touched each photo, praying for the family member or friend pictured there.

She prayed for guidance for her nephew, as he finished college and searched for the job that would best serve God. She prayed for strength and comfort for her sister whose husband had died of a heart attack, leaving her alone and bewildered. She prayed for a wayward brother. On and on she prayed for each personal need.

Next, she pulled the map over in front of her and began praying for different countries as she traced the outline of that country with her fingertip. She prayed for the missionaries working there and the people who would hear the Word of God through them. She prayed for the leadership of the country. Finally, she prayed for spiritual awakening and peace.

I was forever changed that night. For the rest of my life, whenever I strayed away from God, I'd see Aunt Wanda touching my old school picture and calling out my name to God. That memory had a way of pulling me back to the straight and narrow.

And now, years later, my family's pictures are becoming worn from my fingerprints, and of course I have a big tattered map of the world. How else could I remember the names of all those countries when I pray?

Kelly's Hill

Edie Postill Cole

I s it Saturday morning?" I asked as my mother entered my sister's and my bedroom.

"Yes, it's Saturday morning—and yes, Daddy will be home today," she said with a smile.

"Oh, goody! Can we go to meet him?"

"It's pretty cold. We'll see what it's like later."

This same conversation took place many times in years gone by when I was a little girl. We lived in a small village eight miles from the farm, close to my sister's school. My father drove to the farm in the warm, lazy days of summer. But once rains and snow came, he had to walk back and forth.

Monday mornings were always sad as we watched our daddy sling a gunny sack full of groceries over his shoulder and trudge off to the farm. We would stand at the front window and watch him get farther and farther away. It wasn't until he disappeared over the hill that we slowly returned to the day's activities.

The week would drag by, but then it was Saturday and all our gloom vanished! Daddy would be home today!

My sister and I loved to meet him along the way. All day we would wait for our mother to decide if we could. If it wasn't too cold, she would bundle us up in our warmest clothes. A wool scarf encircled my head with only a small slit left so I could peer out at the snowy world around us.

My heart raced as we started on our hike. My stubby legs could hardly maneuver in the deep snow drifts. I clung to my big sister's hand, and she encouraged me and pulled me along with her.

East of our village was a fairly steep hill—Kelly's Hill. We would struggle to the top, huffing and puffing, spurred on by the thought of who we hoped to see once we reached the top.

"Can you see him?" I asked anxiously as we crested the hill.

"Not yet," Doreen replied, searching the horizon.

Finally we could make out the form of one lone figure plodding along in the distance.

"It's him! It's him!" I shouted, jumping up and down in the snow. When the figure got closer, we'd start to run. Daddy would spot us and he'd start to run. He would open his huge arms and both of us would leap into them, laughing and squealing as he hugged and kissed us—one more joyous reunion.

My father, mother, and sister are in heaven now, and when I envision my own arrival there, I think about those Saturday mornings on Kelly's Hill. This time, Jesus will run to meet me first —and I will leap into His open arms, laughing and basking in His love. Then my family will spot me and they'll rush toward me with arms wide open. What a joyous reunion! And this time, there will be no more good-byes.

Breakfast with the Polar Bears

Allison Harms

I went to college when my son went to kindergarten. I had more homework than he did, but we shared the field trips—I chaperoned his class to the fire station and the farm and he joined my class for a couple of fossil hunts and glacier hikes. Once, for one of my biology classes, I was required to visit the zoo on my own sometime during the fall term. I put if off for weeks, waiting for Indian Summer, busy with our new back-to-school schedules. Finally I realized that the end of the term was approaching and I hadn't completed the assignment. I chose a day for the zoo excursion. Of course my son came along too.

It wasn't a typical day at the zoo. The late fall, too early winter weather kept it deserted except for my son and me. Even the animals seemed scarce. Clouds closed down the sky and spat rain that felt like ice needles. Damp gusts eddied around our legs, catching up shredded leaves, paper bags, candy wrappers and peanut shells in a whirlpool of compost at the corner of the reptile house. Only a few eerie fluorescent lights glowed inside. We walked on. The fountains were drained, the garden beds left desolate, the boulevards empty. Ducks huddled together on the lee side of the lake, heads tucked under their wings. Tiny waves smacked the shore. As we walked, the wind filled then flattened our coats against our bodies.

Our footfalls on the paved walk alerted the gazelles at their grazing. A herd of sharp heads, ears, and horns poised like a ballet troupe on tiptoe as we passed. In the distance, we heard the elephant's bugle. The lion's amber eyes followed us; his tufted tail flicked once against the floor. The surface of the hippopotamus' pool winked and the matron lifted her bobbin snout and blinked her liquid eye. The giraffe cocked his head and stared gravely.

We stopped to watch the polar bears. They marched with cool, lumbering strides but their gait was comically bow legged and pigeon-toed. They had overgrown puppies' paws fringed with curved, black claws. Muzzles up, they sniffed the air, swinging their too small, bullet heads from side-to-side and snorting dragon-curls of steam against the cement sky. The scent of snow was as comforting to them as a sunbath for a house cat.

Their keeper came around the corner wearing rubber boots and swinging two red buckets. At their first sight of him, the bears began to plunge into the pool with the rumbling chaos of boulders in an avalanche. They clambered out again, water streaming from their bodies like snowmelt from the mountains.

The keeper walked over to where my son and I stood.

"Good morning," we said to each other. I asked him what was in the buckets.

"Mackerel and watermelon."

"Is that what bears eat for breakfast?" my son asked.

"Yep," the keeper answered. Then bending down to my son's height, he said, "Like to help me feed the bears?"

"Wow! Can I, Mom?"

And so we did, tossing dark wedges of fish and mottled melon rinds into winter's first breath of snow.

Too soon it was time to leave. My son was tired so I carried him in my arms, his hood pulled over his ears, his face pressed into my shoulder. I smiled to myself as I thought of how often the "have tos" in my life turned into "get tos": I had to go to the zoo; I got to spend the day with my son *and* feed breakfast to the polar bears. Doing what's right has rewards of its own. But I could remember so many times when I'd fulfilled an obligation or followed through on a promise even when it cost me to keep it, and something new had opened up for me: a relationship, a skill, an unforgettable moment. And even on the blustery November day, I knew that the memory of our simple, unexpected experience—breakfast with the polar bears—would warm us deep down inside every time we remembered it.

Mothers, don't ever forget the permanence of your imprint. The kids may seem ungrateful, they may act irresponsible, they may even ignore your reminders and forget your advice. But believe this—they cannot erase your influence.

Charles R. Swindoll
from The Finishing Touch

The First Birthday Party

Kathleen Ruckman

I blew up balloons, hung crepe paper streamers across our kitchen doorway, and wondered, *Is this worth all the effort? She won't remember anyway.* I recalled the words of Elnora, my husband's mother: "No one has ever given me a birthday party."

Actually, we had given Elnora a party every year. But Alzheimer's disease had crept in and robbed Elnora not only of the ability to remember her own birthdays but also of the certainty that we loved her and gave parties for her. She would often say, "I never see you," even though we saw her twice a week. I struggled to accept her forgetfulness. This was difficult for me, especially in the beginning when we weren't sure yet of the diagnosis.

I asked God to give me more patience and understanding. God answered my prayer by bringing inspiration from a most unexpected source—Elnora herself.

In earlier days, Elnora and I had exchanged prayer requests. However, once the Alzheimer's disease worsened, I had quit asking her to pray—that is, until my mother was diagnosed with cancer. I will never forget the day I asked Elnora to pray over the phone with me for my mother.

Among our many telephone prayers, I particularly remember that one. Her prayer made sense, and her words flowed without her usual confusion, expressing genuine compassion and sadness.

My mother lived to have two more summer visits with us in Oregon. Though Elnora was declining because of her disease, I once again asked her to pray after I had returned from my mother's funeral. As we sat at my kitchen table, Elnora took my hands in hers and prayed that God would be with me and with the rest of my family.

I "peeked" like a child during Elnora's prayer. Her eyes squinted tightly as she prayed from her heart. That's what I remember most—the earnest expression of one who loved my mother and one who loved the Lord. Her words were beautifully said—almost eloquent. Tears in her eyes lingered after her prayer—but soon confusion returned. Within moments, she forgot my mother had died.

How could this be? In some wonderful way, the spirit and mind must be separate—and Elnora must still know God. Even when she no longer recognized her family, she recognized her God. She communicated with Him in her heart—even when she could no longer talk to us. She was seen by nurses' aides kneeling and praying at her bedside—with her hands folded—at the end of difficult days.

• • •

I hung a few more streamers, deep in thought. I placed the heart-shaped cake I had baked on the center of my kitchen table. Surely her spirit would grasp the love we would give her. I hung a sign that read, "Happy Birthday, Mom. We love you." I could hardly wait for Elnora's party! I wanted this birthday party—the one Elnora would think of as her first—to be very special.

Dad Coming Home
Was the Real Treat

Howard Mann

H hen I was a little boy I never left the house without kissing my parents good-bye.
I liked kissing my mother because her cheek felt mushy and warm, and because she smelled of peppermints. I liked kissing my father because he felt rough and whiskery and smelled of cigars and witch hazel.

About the time I was ten years old, I came to the conclusion that I was now too big to kiss my father. A mother, OK. But with a father, a big boy should shake hands—man to man, you see.

He didn't seem to notice the difference or to mind it. Anyway, he never said anything about it. But then he never said much about anything except his business.

In retrospect, I guess it was also my way of getting even with him. Up until then I had always felt I was something special to him. Every day, he would come home from that mysterious world of his with a wondrous treat, just for me. It might be a miniature baseball bat, engraved with Babe Ruth's signature. It might be a real honeycomb with waffle-like squares soaked in honey. Or it might be exotic rahat, the delectable, jellied Turkish candies, buried in powdered sugar and crowded into a little wooden crate.

How I looked forward to his coming home each night! The door flung open and there he stood. I would run to him, hug him while he lifted me high in his arms.

I reached my peak the day of my seventh birthday. I woke up before anyone else in the family and tiptoed into the dining room. There, on the heavy mahogany table, was a small, square wristwatch with a brown leather strap, stretched out full length in a black velvet box. Could it really be for me? I picked it up and held it to my ear. It ticked! Not a toy watch from the five-and-dime, but a real watch like grown-ups wore. I ran into his bedroom, woke up father and covered him with kisses. Could any boy possibly be as happy as me?

Later, it began to change. At first, I wasn't aware it was happening. I suppose I was too busy with school and play and having to make new friends all the time. (We moved every two years, always seeking a lower rent.)

The flow of treats dried up. No more bats or honeycombs. My father gradually disappeared from my life. He would come home late, long after I had gone to sleep. And he would come home with his hands empty. I missed him very much, but I was afraid to say anything. I hoped that he would come back to me as strangely as he had left. Anyhow, big boys weren't supposed to long for their fathers.

Years after he died, my mother talked about how the Depression had "taken the life out of him." It had crushed his dream of being a "big man." He no longer had money for treats. He no longer had time for me.

I am sorry now. I look at his picture and his crinkly hazel eyes and wish that he were here today. I would tell him what is happening with me now and talk about things that he might like to hear—politics, foreign events and how business is doing. And I would put my arms around his neck and say, "Pop, you don't have to bring me anything—just come home early."

And I would kiss him.

Leaving Home

John Trent
from Love for All Seasons

High school was over, and I'd been up almost all night, first saying good-bye to my few remaining high school friends and then packing for college myself. Now I sat at our old kitchen table with my mother, enjoying her famous pancakes one last time before climbing into my jam-packed car. As I sat at that table, a flood of emotions hit me.

My mother had purchased the table when I was five years old. It sat next to a large kitchen window, with a commanding view of the front yard. For more than a decade, it served as the unofficial meeting place of the Trent family. In grade school, I can remember sitting there at countless dinners. There would be us three boys laughing and chattering about our day, my mother and grandmother scurrying back and forth to keep bottomless plates filled, and my grandfather quietly presiding over the chaos.

In high school, that table became the place where I could sit with my mother, anytime, day or night. There she would patiently listen to whatever "crisis" or problem I was having in school or in dating. That old table proudly displayed birthday cards as we grew older and solemnly bore the flowers we brought home from the funeral home the day my grandfather was laid to rest.

Over the years, more chairs began to empty. My older brother, Joe, married and began a home of his own. My grandmother went to live with my aunt, and my twin brother, Jeff, left for a different college. Now it was down to just Mom and me, sitting at that table one last time.

I can remember how well I thought she was handling that

morning. No tears. No dip in her always present smile. Just that nonstop encouragement that has calmed my fears since I was a child and always made me feel like I could accomplish anything I set my mind to. Things like driving a thousand miles by myself to a new college and making a new start without knowing a single person at an out-of-state school.

I finished breakfast, hugged the best mom in the world, and confidently strode to my '64 forest green Volkswagen. Every square inch was crammed with "important stuff" for college—everything from my legendary record collection to my new, seldom-used razor. I jumped inside the car, fired up the engine, and drove off with a wave and a smile. I was on my way! Nothing was going to stop me now! Nothing, that is, except driving into the rising sun that quickly made me realize I'd forgotten one thing—my sunglasses on the night stand.

I turned the car around, drove back into the driveway, and walked in to find my mother still sitting at the kitchen table, *crying*. All morning she had kept a stiff upper lip, managing to hold her emotions in check at seeing her last son leave home. But when I walked back in the door unexpectedly, all that changed. There was an awkward silence, and then we both lost it. We sat at that table, crowded with memories, hugged each other, and cried and cried.

I can't explain exactly what happened that sun-splashed morning in the kitchen, but our relationship changed. There was no less love, no less caring, but somehow we both knew that this would be the last time I would sit down at that old kitchen table as a child.

Sister Dresses

Faith Andrews Bedford

As my sister's car disappears over the top of the hill, her faint toot in farewell tells me she has turned onto the main road. The dust settles on our lane and I look to the pile of boxes she just left behind.

When Mother died last year, Dad gave up the summer house.

"Come and take what you want, girls," he had said to us, and we did.

I chose the tall secretary where Mother sat so often writing letters by a sunny window. Beth chose a painting of the summer house itself. Ellen picked a statue of horses, for she and Mother had shared a love of riding. After the moving van left with the things that Dad wanted, my sisters and I had lingered in the cottage going through drawers full of old letters, boxes of slides, albums of faded photos—the collective memory of a family. We had put it all into a dozen boxes and each of us chose four. Now Beth has dropped off my boxes; Ellen's house is her next stop.

I sit down on the top step of the porch and open a box marked "albums." Here are photographs of my father, resplendent in his Navy uniform, and one of my mother leaning against their first car. There is a faded picture of the family gathered for my christening, the women elegant in hats and gloves, the men's faces shadowed by their fedoras. As I slowly leaf through the pages, the family grows, we buy our first house, the cars get bigger. Then, there on the last page, is the picture of us in our sister dresses.

I can almost feel the starched ruffles and hear the rustle of the crinolines that were needed to keep the skirts nice and full. I remember Mother's delight when she found these dresses at the children's shop in the village. There was one in my size and one for Ellen but no size four for Beth. We were so excited when Mrs. Page, the shopkeeper, told us she felt sure she could order one for Beth that would come in time for Easter.

When the big box arrived in early April we gathered around Mother as she lifted the dresses out one by one. The pink tissue paper rustled as she held each one up. They were made of clouds of dotted Swiss—white organdy with blue-flocked dots. The skirt and collar were trimmed with tiny blue bows.

"To match your eyes," Mother had said.

We were allowed to try them on just once so that we could have a "fashion show" for Father that evening. As we twirled into the dining room in our new finery, he burst into applause. Ellen and I daintily grasped the ruffled skirts and executed our best curtsies; Beth scrunched her dress up in her chubby little hands and made a close approximation of one, almost toppling over in the process. Then we had to carefully hang our finery up until Easter Sunday.

As I look at the photograph, I can recall the warmth of the pale spring sunshine on our faces that day. We undoubtedly resisted putting on coats to go to church. They surely would have crushed those beautiful dresses and besides, how then could anyone have seen how wonderfully we matched?

In time, I handed my dress down to Ellen and she handed hers down to Beth. Finally, only Beth had one of those beautiful dresses, its bow a bit bedraggled after countless wearings by three little girls. But those dotted Swiss dresses were only the beginning of a long parade of matching sister outfits. Mother obviously was so pleased with the effect that she began an Easter tradition. I remember the year of the blue calicoes and the year we all had matching yellow jumpers. Even Father got into the spirit of things when he came back from a business trip to Arizona with Mexican dresses for each of his girls—even Mother.

Those wonderful white dresses with rows and rows of bright ribbons edging the wide collars and hems, and skirts that were cut in a complete circle. Father put Ravel's *Bolero* on the record player and we spun madly about the living room, our beribboned skirts fluttering like crazed butterflies. At last we crashed, giggling, into a heap. Dad, quite pleased with our reaction to his gift, sat in his armchair and grinned his "that's-my-girls" smile.

As I look at the photograph, I remember these very first sister dresses so clearly that I am somewhat surprised that I cannot remember the last ones. Maybe Mother knew we were outgrowing the idea. Perhaps it was I who, at the sophisticated age of 14, first protested, saying something like, "Really, Mother, I'm much too old for that sort of thing."

Gradually, as we grew older, I think Mother saw how very different we all were becoming and just stopped buying us matching dresses.

By the time we were in our 20s, our lives were on three very distinct tracks. Our wardrobes clearly reflected our different worlds. Mother would shake her head in bemused bewilderment and say to Father, "How did we get three daughters so different?" He would merely smile.

Though our lives have continued to run along different pathways, the circle draws closer as we grow older and once again realize how similar we are. Now we are all mothers, equally challenged by our various roles. And although our wardrobes still differ widely, we all seem to be moving toward variations on "classic." Last Christmas I gave all the women in the family silk blouses. Same style, different colors. Everyone loved them.

Mother didn't realize what a tradition she started. When my own daughters were little, I often made them sister dresses.

When I was expecting my third child, I made myself a maternity dress out of some bright pink cotton. Eleanor, my elder daughter, loved the fabric, so I made a jumper for her out of the scraps. That baby turned out to be a girl. So, in a way, my daughters' sister dresses started even before birth.

For as long as I can remember, Dad had always given Mother a beautiful nightgown each Christmas. They were long and silky with plenty of lace. When we were little, we used to love to stroke their satiny smoothness. With Mother gone, we knew that tradition would stop. Christmas was bittersweet this year. The tree certainly sparkled, but there was no big pink box from "Sweet Dreams" beneath it.

We put on happy faces for the sake of our children, but all the little touches that Mother always added to Christmas were missing. Suddenly Ellen drew out from behind the tree three identical white boxes. On the lids, written in Dad's bold hand, were the words "From the Nightie Gnome." We opened them and lifted out three identical red flannel nightshirts.

We whooped with delight as we pulled them out of the tissue paper, then ran down the hall to put them on. When we came back into the living room to show off our sister nighties, Dad had put Ravel's *Bolero* on the stereo. We joined hands and did an impromptu dance. As the music grew louder, we twirled around faster and faster ignoring the widening eyes of our disbelieving husbands and the gaping mouths of our children.

I smile now at the sight we must have made: three grown women dressed in red flannel nighties whirling madly through a jumble of empty boxes and wrapping paper. When the music ended in a clash of cymbals, we crashed, giggling, into a heap.

Our husbands shook their heads in wonder. The younger children nearly keeled over with embarrassment while the older ones held their sides with laughter. Dad just cracked his "that's-my-girls" grin.

The Safe House

Margaret Jensen
from A View from the Top

Within the hollow of a cave, the mountain of stone cradled a simple frame house and red barn. From the rocky ledge the cottage looked down from the mountain to the clear-flowing fjord. There was only one view—the forward look, with towering mountains overlooking the narrow arm of the sea that ran between the walls of stone.

Protected from the storms, the sturdy cottage looked snug and safe. For a moment I imagined that I was part of that safe house, just a speck surrounded by the majestic beauty of Norway, the Land of the Midnight Sun. Patches of green revealed garden spots for food, while down the mountain the fish swam in the cold, blue water. Hidden in the cleft of the rock of my imagination I dared to dream of a long-ago time when my people came from the Land of the Midnight Sun.

In the cave of my imagination I wondered if there had been a little girl who looked like my youngest granddaughter, Kathryn Elise, with long corn-silk hair and deep blue eyes. Perhaps there had been a "Katie" with a vivid imagination, who curled up on a rocky ledge and dreamed of faraway places beyond the mountains. Did she dream of writing books or of putting the mountains, sky, and sea on canvas with her brush and oil? How often did she descend the stone steps to fish with her father or climb back to tend gardens, goats, and chickens? Could she have dreamed that down the corridors of time someone would sail in ships to the then-unknown world called America?

Today our Katie knows that her great-great-grandparents came to this land and that I, her "Grammy," was the first in the

Tweten family to be born in Woodville, Wisconsin, USA, in 1916.

Today I look into the next century, the year 2000, and back again over the years. Somehow deep within me I desire to face Home—not the little house nestled in the arms of stone, or my lovely home surrounded by flowers, but the Home where the Father has a prepared place cradled in the arms of His love. I may not see the next century, but I will see my eternal Home.

We speak of the valley of the shadow of death, but I see the mountain of hope, with the lights of Home reflected over the rocky climb. Generations have preceded me; friends and loved ones waved good-bye with a sigh and a smile—a sight to leave the familiar but a smile of hope for the eternal. It's been a long climb, these 80-plus years; faith sees my eternal Home more real than my lovely home of brick and wood.

With the morning dew still on my roses I open the screen door to walk into the morning sun. From the patio swing, with my coffee cup in hand, I watch the squirrels and dog chase each other across the green grass. In the brisk ocean breeze I watch the pampas grass waltz in the wind, while the palm trees bow gracefully in a French minuet. The sassy daisies with bold dark eyes jitterbug to the music of the early morning. Birds in the treetops sing their song and keep the orchestra off-key.

Periwinkles, my favorites, look up at me with gentle faces that say, "We'll be here, the last to leave when winter winds blow—but come spring, we'll arrive early." Faithful—always faithful! Sun, wind, cold, rain, or heat, their faces look up with a smile. "We are here for you."

The roses wilt, the gladioli bend in the storm; even the sturdy marigold turns brown; the geranium needs attention; the happy red salvia get discouraged, and their petals fall. Not my periwinkles! They greet me with *faithfulness*. Up and down the mountain of life, into the valley of broken hearts, up the rocky climb, over stumps and briars, the periwinkle people keep coming—

climbing, falling, stumbling, sliding, they keep coming.

How God must love the periwinkle people—the *faithful ones!*

I put my coffee cup down and walk along, pulling a weed here and there, toward the 45 yucca bushes I planted along the road. The prickly yucca serves a purpose, to keep out stray animals—a fortress of pricks, but not for a centerpiece.

Talking to my Doberman, Scout, is a front for talking with Harold, my husband of 53 years, who died several years ago. I don't usually tell that, but it is true. Walking through the garden I ask, "Do you remember when we planted 30 holly bushes— look how they have grown!" (He remembers.)

"Remember how we planted the azaleas in pouring rain, then dug holes for the pampas grass we got on sale for $1?" (I'm sure he remembers.)

"Look at the palm trees and how they withstood the hurricane." (I'm sure he peeked between the clouds.)

"No one is around, so I can talk to you, Harold. Sometimes in the evening I cry—especially when I sit at the piano and sing the old love songs: "Oh how I miss you tonight, miss you when the lights are low...." That seems to be the hardest time, when I turn on the lights and close the blinds. I seem to see you in your leather chair.

"But they aren't tears of grief, guilt, or regret, just those 'missing you' kind of tears, because hope lets me see the lights of Home. I have two homes, Harold—the one you prepared on earth (and thank you for all your hard work, painting, and planting) and another Home where the heart lives."

With a thankful heart I walk away from the palm tree that bent and swayed under hurricane winds but stood up to welcome a new day when the sun came out.

Grandparents

PICTURE PERFECT

If your baby is "beautiful and perfect,
never cries or fusses,
sleeps on schedule and burps on demand,
an angel all the time"
...you're the grandma.

Teresa Bloomingdale
from Letting Go

Inheritance Day

Philip Gulley
from Hometown Tales

I n the autumn of my grandfather's ninety-second year, he moved to a retirement home. The decision to move had been a long time in the making. Grandma had died two years earlier. He was afraid that closing the door to their home one last time would make their good-bye permanent. Complicating the decision was their dog, Babe, who was going with him no matter what. Dispensing the family heirlooms was the final hurdle—the kitchen table he'd built from a wind-shook cherry tree in 1941, Grandma's mahogany bed, and the woodworking tools.

Since childhood, I had shown a penchant for tools of all types. I spent a fair portion of my youth perched on Grandpa's workshop stool, eyeing his implements and learning about their upkeep.

"Delta-Milwaukee drill press, built in 1939," he instructed. "Oil it once a month. Craftsman table saw. Don't ever buy a new one; just buy another motor when the old one goes bad. These are carving knives. Keep them sharp. A dull knife is a dangerous knife."

Then the most beautiful words of all to my young ears: "Someday these tools will be yours."

I could scarcely wait for them to be mine, not thinking how receiving them would signal Grandpa's final days. Whenever I visited him, I would finger the tools, imagining them in my workshop. But as I grew older and my affection for Grandpa increased, my yearning for his tools diminished. I began to realize they would be bought at a heavy price.

A week before he entered the retirement home, he invited

me to his house. "Bring a truck," he said. I arrived the next morning with my friend Jim. Grandpa hobbled out to his workshop, and I followed. Jim had the good sense to linger in the background. Grandpa unlatched the door and we made our way inside.

He rested his hand on the drill press. "This is a 1939 Delta-Milwaukee drill press," he told me. "You'll need to oil it once a month." He worked his way through to the carving knives. "Remember to keep these sharp. A dull knife is a dangerous knife."

It was a sober morning.

My wife and I unloaded the tools that evening and carried them to my basement workshop. I arranged them just so while my little boy Spencer looked on from his perch on the workshop stool.

"This was Grandpa's drill press," I told him. "Now it belongs to me. And these are carving knives. When you're bigger I'll show you how to use them."

He looked up at me from the stool. "Can I have them?"

"Yes, Spencer, someday a long time from now, when Daddy doesn't need them anymore, these tools will be yours."

He grinned a shy grin. Those were beautiful words to his young ears.

Forty-five years from now, I'll totter out to my workshop with son in tow. It will be his Inheritance Day. I will have oiled the drill press once a month, just as Grandpa taught me to do. It will be one hundred years old and will work just fine. My son's friend will linger in the background, while Spencer and I go over the tools' upkeep one last time. "Don't forget, son, a dull knife is a dangerous knife."

I wonder if on that day my son will feel the melancholy I felt on my Inheritance Day. I wonder if he'll lie awake on that distant night, wishing his daddy was still long for this world, as I wish that now of Grandpa.

Late at night, when my sons are asleep and my wife is

reading in her chair, I go down to my workshop and think of grandpas and daddies and sons and the faithful rhythm of it all.

The reason God made grandmas is they are sweet,
they comfort you when you're down—
and most of all—because they love you.

Breanah Shantel Gray, age 8

Dinner Out

Maryann Lee Jacob

We went to a little cafe
    just off the campus
    to have a quiet dinner together
    the college students there
    eating, discussing deep philosophical issues.

You sat at our table
    looking suave and debonair in jeans and turtleneck,
    your tousled hair shining,
    your eyes sparkling, full of mischief.
And you worked your charms
    on me and everyone around.

The waitress doted on you,
    your cup always filled
    "An extra napkin? Certainly!"
    "More crackers for your soup? Of course!"
    You flirted notoriously with her
    and with the hostess as well,
    flashing seductive grins at them,
    inviting them to talk,
    eating only the fringes of your meal.

Twice you left our table
    to walk around
    and spread your charms elsewhere,
    stopping at a table or two,
    grinning broadly, flirtatiously,
    soliciting conversation.

I watched you captivate their hearts
   and knew you had taken mine,
   as I sat quietly observing.

Finally, folding my dinner napkin patiently
   and placing it beside my finished plate,
   I knew it was time to go,
   and walking up to you I said,
   "Let's say good-bye."

And picking you up, I placed you
   in your stroller,
   and as we left,
   you waved profusely at everyone,
   after your first dinner out with Grandma,
   when you were only two.

A Summer Smile

Hester Tetreault

Rebecca ran a comb through her hair, scanned the reflection in the mirror and mentally stamped her approval. "Don't forget to stop by Grandma's on your way. The magazines are by the door," her mother called.

Rebecca groaned. She let the door bang behind her. She felt rushed, inconvenienced, and in the car she applied a heavy foot to the accelerator. Maybe she could still make it to youth group on time.

Grandma was in the garden tending her roses when Rebecca pulled up to the curb. "Hi, Grandma," she shouted, compensating for the impaired hearing in her grandmother's left ear.

Grandma straightened with deliberate care and winced, but her face lit up. "Come on in, Rebecca dear."

"I can't, Grandma. I'm running late. I'll leave the magazines on the hall table."

A flicker of disappointment displaced Grandma's smile. Inside, the aroma of baking made Rebecca glance through to the kitchen. Cookies cooled on a rack. She felt bad, then cross, for having to feel that way. "Sorry I can't stay, Grandma," she grimaced, "but it's youth group tonight, and I'm already running late."

Bumping her forehead with the palm of her hand, Grandma gave a little laugh. "Of course it is. One day runs into the next, and I don't always keep them straight. Don't let me make you late, Honey."

"Thanks, Grandma." She deposited a peck on Grandma's cheek and jumped into the car. "I'll see you Sunday," she called, compensating for the hasty departure. Most Sundays

Grandma joined them for dinner. Mother said she had a better appetite when she ate with the family. Generally, Grandma came to church with them, too, but lately she hadn't been well enough. Whenever Rebecca's mother expressed concern, Grandma would only say, "I'll feel better when summer comes."

Colleen greeted Rebecca in the church parking lot. "Guess who'll be in town the weekend after next?"

Rebecca knew by the tone of her voice it had to be Jeff. She felt her face flush...Jeff was more than a girlish crush to her; she'd known him since seventh grade. He was four years her senior. The first time she'd shown up to the junior high church group, practically forced there by her parents, he'd rescued her. He'd greeted her, gathered her in, made her feel part of the group, all before she could give in to the irresistible urge to take flight. Jeff had gone away to college. She was now a senior in high school. Did she just imagine it, or had he really stopped treating her like a kid during his visits home?

That thought remained uppermost in her mind when, Saturday, she readied herself to go to the clearance sale at the mall. Maybe she'd find something really cool and sophisticated to wear the weekend he was home. "While you're out today," her mother interjected, "could you stop and pick up a couple of things for Grandma at the drug store? There's a prescription and..."

It wasn't the errand. It was knowing that Grandma would want to talk and visit, no telling how long that would take. "Mom," she sighed, "I'm too busy. I'm meeting Colleen. I have tons to do, and..."

"Okay," her mother interrupted. "I'll do it." The hint of disdain in her voice made Rebecca want to defend herself, "Anyway," her mother continued, making a defense unnecessary, "There's bound to be some things I can help Grandma with, if I go."

Rebecca helped with dinner preparations that evening. It had been a great day. She'd found the perfect dress and a pair of jeans, both fifty percent off the mark down price! She felt amiable, chatty even. Her mother liked it when she was in the mood to talk. "We're going downtown to help serve dinner at the homeless shelter next month. Oh! and Friday we're going to the nursing home again." She remembered her first visit to the nursing home. What a shock it had been, the frailty and hopelessness compounded by the concentration of so much old age under one roof. But she didn't feel awkward visiting any more, and the musty, clinical smell was no longer offensive. She had learned it was important to listen, to hold unsteady hands, and hug bent and bony frames. "Honestly, Mom, it can be such a depressing place. I'm so glad Grandma isn't in a place like that." Her mother cast one of her whimsical, wise looks that made Rebecca feel like she'd missed something.

Colleen linked arms with Rebecca as they crossed the parking lot after youth group the following Wednesday. "Wasn't it great tonight?" Colleen said. "Did you see that new guy in the back again this week? I think he's going to stick around. He's cute. Besides," she added reflectively, "he is so intense, like he's there for the right reasons. I like that in a guy. Are you okay?"

Rebecca had been staring at the ground. She jerked her head to meet Colleen's gaze. "I'm fine. Really. I'm fine."

Alone in her room she felt anything but fine. The youth pastor's message had left her strangely disquieted. The song really got to her, too, something about hurting those you love and passing them by. Snatches of conversation emerged—a look, a smile—Grandma's smile that tucked disappointments behind it. She could feel Grandma's soft, wrinkled cheek as she brushed hurried kisses against it. She thought of her vein-streaked, arthritic hand stirring cookie dough. Then she remembered her mother's look that made her know she'd missed something in the midst of all her youthful wisdom. How could she have been so blind? When was the last time she actually sat down with Grandma without needing to rush off to something else?

In bed she listened to the wind rustling the leaves outside her window and recalled nights snuggled up on Grandma's couch listening to stories. She remembered feeling tall as she stood on a stool beside Grandma in the kitchen. She had been the one to struggle with the heavy dough then. When Grandma taught her to knit, how patiently she retrieved lost stitches no matter how many times her own small fingers dropped them.

Tears trickled down her cheeks. She did care about others, truly she did, but it was tainted, influenced by pride and fun and friends. Why had she allowed so much activity to crowd out someone who had loved her all these years? "I'm so sorry, Lord. I Ielp me make it up to Grandma."

The next morning, standing under the hot shower, she hummed the song that had spoken such conviction. She stopped with a sudden sense of wonder. The heaviness was gone. She felt loved, and she longed to reach out to her grandmother with the love God poured into her. The song, it seemed, had become the prayer of her heart.

It poured with rain on Friday. Saturday was overcast. Rebecca stopped by her grandmother's house. "No matter what happens, Grandma, we will spend Sunday afternoon together," she vowed.

"You had a call," her Mother told her when she got home. Rebecca's heart skipped when she saw Jeff's name. "I'll call from upstairs."

"I'm home for the weekend. I was wondering...if you're free tomorrow afternoon, would you like to drive to the beach after church?"

His voice faded. She had dreamed of this day. She wanted to say "yes" so badly. She remembered the anticipation on her grandmother's face. "Jeff, I'd love to go," she struggled, "but I'm taking my grandmother to Pine Creek tomorrow afternoon." She stifled a deep sigh, hoping fervently that he understood.

Sunday emerged warm and clear. In the afternoon, wisps of white streaked across a blue sky. Rebecca stretched out to tan her arms and legs in the thin May sun. Grandma sat with a car blanket tucked around her lap. Rebecca smiled when Grandma declared the sandwiches to be the best she'd ever tasted. "Delicate" was how Rebecca tried to make them. Grandma liked thinly sliced bread with thinly sliced something in between, and always the crusts removed.

She was sitting on Grandma's "good" side which helped, but Rebecca found she didn't have to shout, or repeat herself. The solitude possessed a quietness all its own, seeming to carry conversation between them. After a while conversation became punctuations in long moments of silent companionship. They sat by the creek watching the water tumble over the rocks while chickadees flitted amongst the overhanging branches.

Rebecca looked at the relaxed, blanketed figure. Suddenly she was confronted by her grandmother's frailty and the reality that she would not always be there to love. Was it something in her face? Her eyes perhaps? She reached for her grandmother's hand. "Remember all the things we used to do together when I was little?"

"I certainly do, Honey. I expect I remember a lot more than you," Grandma chuckled, patting her hand. "I remember you hiding under the covers in the guest room, pretending to be asleep, when it was time to go home."

"Grandma. How come my nightgown was always under the pillow and the bed was so cozy?"

Grandma lowered her eyes sheepishly. "Because I wanted you to stay just as much as you did, and I'd have it ready. In the winter I put the electric blanket on so it would be warm for you."

Rebecca laughed at the joint conspiracy, then grew serious. "I've neglected you, Grandma. I've been so wrapped up in my own activities, and..."

Grandma patted her arm. "Now don't you go feeling bad. It's natural at your age. Of course I want to see you...It can be lonely at my age. I can't do things like I used to, and, well, little things become important, but I forget just how busy young folks are. It's easy for me to become self-centered and demanding." She smiled knowingly. "The Lord talks to me too, you know."

Rebecca studied her dear face for a moment. She hadn't outgrown her grandmother. She needed her as much as ever. There was no generation gap. They were two women, one old and wise, the other young and full of possibilities.

They talked as they walked along the path by the creek. Grandma leaned on her arm for support, pausing often to catch her breath and "look at the view." Her eyes were bright, and there was a hint of pink in her cheeks. Even her hands were warm.

For Rebecca the warmth of the sun matched the warmth inside. She hadn't anticipated the joy and contentment this day would bring. She inhaled it until, quite magically, she felt suspended in time. She was glad she had been able to say "no" to Jeff. Somehow she knew there would be another invitation. "I love you very much, Grandma. I'm so glad we spent this day together."

Grandma squeezed her arm. There was a slight tremor in her voice. "I am, too, dear." She paused to study a flock of birds swooping high in the sky, took a deep breath and smiled. It was a smile with contentment tucked behind it, and when she spoke it was with determination. "You know, Rebecca dear, I do believe summer has finally come."

Grandpa and Me

Jordan, age 9

The dad in my life isn't really my dad, he's my grandpa. But he's been like a dad to me since before I was born. Four months before I was born my real father left my mommy. My grandpa drove four hundred miles to come get my mommy and me. He took care of my mommy until I was born. When I came home from the hospital there was a cradle that Grandpa made just for me. Someday, my kids will sleep in the same cradle.

When I was a baby I cried a lot at night. Grandpa would walk me around and around the kitchen table. He rocked me to sleep and he was my first baby-sitter.

Now I'm nine years old and Grandpa is my best buddy. We do lots of things together. We go to zoos, museums, and parks. We watch baseball games on TV and we have Chex Mix together—just the two of us.

When I was four my grandpa spent a whole summer building me a playhouse with a big sandbox underneath. He made me a tire swing and pushed me lots of times in it. He pushed me real high, way up over his head. Now he spends all his extra time building new rooms on our house so that Mommy and I will have our own apartment. If we didn't live at Grandpa's house we would have to live in a little apartment in town and I couldn't have my dog, my two house cats, my barn cats, and my gerbils. My grandpa doesn't like cats very much but he lets me keep two cats in the house and he buys lots of cat food and feeds the barn cats even when it's really cold outside.

My grandpa is really patient. When he is busy building things he always takes time to start a nail so that I can pound it in. After he's spent all day mowing our big lawn he is really tired but he will still hook my wagon up to the lawn mower and drive me all over the place.

My grandpa loves Jesus and he wants me to learn about Him, too. Sometimes people on TV talk about kids from single parent families. I'm not one of them because I have three parents in my family. My grandpa isn't my father, but I wouldn't trade him for all the dads in the world.

TREASURES

Today, as a grandfather of six, it is increasingly apparent that my most treasured possessions, next to life in Christ, are the members of my family.... Someday when all is gone, when I can no longer see or hear or talk—indeed when I may no longer know their names—the faces of my loved ones will be on my soul.

Kent Hughes
from Disciplines of a Godly Man

Tea for Two

Emilie Barnes
from If Teacups Could Talk

My granddaughter Christine and I are kindred spirits. We bonded when she was an infant—my first grand-baby. Our relationship has been special ever since, and tea parties have been part of that special relationship.

One Saturday afternoon as we were walking to the mailbox together, ten-year-old Christine said, "Grammy, let's make some scones and have tea."

The next thing I knew, we were in the kitchen whipping up our basic scone recipe. In just a matter of minutes we had popped them in the oven and were setting the table for a simple tea party—just Christine and me.

When the scones were done, we sat down. She poured the tea with practiced ease—we've done this before! We smeared the hot, tasty scones with our favorite jam and whipped topping.

But it's what happened next that made the afternoon so special. Once the tea was poured, we began to talk about friendships, parents, brothers (she has two), and what she could expect as a preadolescent. I was amazed at her knowledge and maturity. We ended up talking about spiritual matters—about God and the meaning of life.

It was only afterward, as I was carefully washing the china cups and returning them to their home in my oak armoire, that I realized what had happened that afternoon: Christine had asked for a tea party.

But what she was really asking for was *time with me.* Asking for tea was her way of saying "I need to talk to you."

Solitude

Erma Bombeck
from Forever Erma

I have always directed my Christmas column toward families who are caught up in a tinsel marathon of tree trimming, stocking stuffing, music making, dogs barking and children squealing.

They're so busy that sometimes I get only a glance before the garbage is wrapped in me. Occasionally, someone puts me on the back porch to catch the slush from boots. If I'm lucky I escape the licking flames when I get thrown into the fireplace with discarded wrappings and warranties.

So I've decided to write to all of you today who have the time to read me: those who have just moved to an area and haven't made new friends...those who are alone because they can't afford the trip home...those whose families have been splintered by distance or disinterest. And you are alone.

Let me tell you about my grandfather. He lived by himself in a little trailer in southwest Ohio until he died a few years ago. I always felt sorry for him when I visited at Christmas because he only had about five cards on top of the TV set, two or three packages at the most to open, and a pitiful artificial tree with a single strand of lights that bubbled like they were going to boil over.

You would have thought those pathetic trappings were straight from the Sistine Chapel.

He'd pick up each card, trace the scene with his fingers and marvel, "This is pretty enough to put in a frame." Then he'd recite the message inside, which he had memorized.

The boxes were another delight. He'd shake them and make a guess as to what they held and place them gently under the tree. Then he'd prime you for that big moment when he said, "I'm going to light the tree for you!" My sewing machine had a bigger light.

The year before he died, when he spent Christmas in the hospital, he raved the entire visiting period over a favor on his dinner tray: a Styrofoam Santa Claus with a red gumdrop hat held on by a toothpick.

Every Christmas since then, I have had to ask myself: Can I quote a single line from the stack of cards I receive? Can I visit without keeping an eye on my watch? Can I become child-like with excitement over a box that obviously holds a handkerchief? Can I live with my solitude without self-pity?

God help me. I think my grandfather felt sorry for me.

Grandpa's Hands

Casandra Lindell

Grandpa's hands were cracked and stained from years of farm work; his left thumb rounded backward, broken by a hammer years before. They were rough and scarred, but they carried warmth and strength.

Only three things mattered to Grandpa: his family, his land, and his God. He was a smart man when it came to practical things and common sense, but he wasn't one for "book learnin'." He never learned to read well. But when I stayed overnight at Grandpa's house I would listen to him and Grandma take turns reading the Bible. Its cover was as worn as the hands that held it. He stumbled over the awkward words, and many times he'd ask Grandma to look up the meaning of a word in the small dictionary they kept nearby. In recent months the dictionary had been misplaced.

Grandpa's hands held countless memories: they taught me to tie my own shoes when I was six years old. Once, a temperamental horse raised its back leg to kick my grandpa and I saw those firm, authoritative hands settle the hoof back to earth with one sharp slap and an abrupt command. I remember hands that scratched skin and snagged clothes when they tickled. Hands that gently cared for my grandmother at home until her death.

He lived and breathed his land. "You know," he once told me as we sat looking at the vineyard from the house, "sometimes people ask what my hobbies are." He nodded his head toward the vines as his eyes softened to look far away. He smiled. "That's my hobby, right out there. I never want to be anywhere else."

His hands were strong, rough, and warm until he died. My last fond memory came the night before his second open heart surgery. We walked through his yard toward the corral to feed the horses. He stopped short and laid one hand on my shoulder, then he pointed to a bush at the edge of the drive. A bird's nest—and I listened for the thousandth time about what a nuisance starlings are to farmers and how loud blue jays shriek early on a summer morning.

Three days later, at the memorial service, I said good-bye to my grandfather by placing a new dictionary, along with his worn Bible, in hands that told so many stories. Inside the Bible were three grape leaves pressed between the pages.

Later that day, I stood at the edge of Grandpa's vineyard. Tears burned up my throat, spilled down my face, and left my insides hollow. Those strong, warm hands had lost their grip on this life but they had taken a stronger hold of the next. The hollow inside began to warm as I watched a handful of the rich soil sift through my own fingers. I brought the earth to my face and inhaled the smell of home. Grandpa never wanted to be anywhere else and in my heart I know that he never will be anywhere else—but home.

Grandma's Laughter

Casandra Lindell

Violets and roses will always be soft, happy flowers to me because they were my grandmother's favorite—and my grandmother always laughed.

Small pots of violets covered a two-level table in the living room. They must have known she loved them because they were always in bloom. I can see her in my mind's eye, carefully picking off spotted leaves and smiling the flowers from their stems. She did the same thing with people—smiling, encouraging, carefully tending.

Roses bordered the entire yard and Grandma tended them carefully with the same smile. Throughout the spring and summer Grandpa regularly cut armfuls of roses for the house. He kept the tables full of bouquets in cut glass vases. Any visitor could count on taking home a handful of roses from the yard.

But visitors took home more than roses—they took home Grandma's laughter. She "got tickled" when she was lost and drove in circles looking for an address. She smiled with warmth to match the main course as she put the last of the evening meal on the table. She laughed in delight as she cuddled me while I told her a story. She giggled when hummingbirds fluttered outside the dining room window.

When Grandma dropped a glass bottle of maple syrup in the grocery store, she smiled and said she felt clumsy. She turned to call someone to clean it up and stepped in the syrup. She slipped, and fell, and broke her wrist. As she lay there on her back, propped on her unbroken arm to keep from lying on a shard of glass, Grandma started laughing. She laughed while the employees helped her up. She laughed as she waited for the ambulance, and she laughed when she told the story even years later.

When she died, my five-year-old nephew wanted to say good-bye, and he didn't quite understand what that meant. My sister told him, the best she could, that he wouldn't be able to sit in Grandma's lap and she wouldn't tell him stories anymore. Tommy drew a picture and his dad helped him write "I'll miss you, Grandma. It's OK to cry" across the top.

"Mommy?" His big eyes were questioning, his brow puzzled. "I won't hear her laughing, will I?"

Like Tommy, I thought I would miss Grandma's laughter most of all.

Until four months later. I sat at Grandma's dining room table, painting a vase as I waited for Grandpa to come home. As I reached to pick up the phone, my sleeve caught the container of black paint and swept it off the table—to land upside down on the carpet.

"That's OK," I heard myself say out loud in a sweet and gentle tone not quite my own. "Clean it up as best you can. It's an old carpet." And then I started laughing. I laughed at my clumsiness and at the black smear that just seemed to spread despite my best efforts. I giggled at the mass of paper towels piling up in the garbage bag. And then I sat back and laughed in delight at a full grown little girl who had learned to *find* delight in even the messiest situations.

I almost looked up to see if Grandma was standing there—and then I realized that Grandma's laughter was still with me.

Grandmas Make a Difference

Betty Southard

The photo studio was packed with mommies in line and kids everywhere. As my daughter waited her turn to see the proofs of the photos taken the week before, I was playing and laughing with Elizabeth, my 18-month-old granddaughter. I soon noticed a little black-haired girl standing alone across the room. Her huge dark eyes never left Elizabeth and me. No one was paying attention to her and my grandmother's heart reached out.

"Hi!" I said. "What's your name?"

The child dropped her head, shuffled her feet and mumbled something softly.

"What?" I asked. "I didn't hear you."

The reaction was the same. I wondered if perhaps she didn't speak English and didn't understand me. I smiled and started to turn my attention back to Elizabeth when the little girl's demeanor suddenly changed.

Holding her head high, standing tall and looking me directly in the eye, she spoke loud and clear: "But Grandma calls me Precious!"

The Holly Trees

Melody Carlson

Whenever I get pricked by holly, I think of Grandpa. My grandfather never liked to waste anything. He was one of those pioneer-spirited men who did everything with his own two hands; relying on his wits and whatever natural materials were nearby to solve a problem. He appreciated a good challenge. I like to think that I might have learned, or inherited, some of that from him.

But back to the holly. Growing up in the sixties wasn't easy when your parents were divorced, and your dad seemed to have disappeared off the face of the planet; especially when everyone else seemed to be living like Ozzie and Harriet. And although my mom worked hard to keep us clothed and fed, when Christmas time rolled around, life suddenly seemed rather bleak and barren. About the time of the school Christmas party, all I could think about was making that three-hour drive to my grandparents' house where Christmas was really Christmas. Where food and relatives abounded; and artificial trees, like the cheesy tin-foil job in our tiny living room, were not allowed. You see, every year, my grandpa cut down a tree tall enough to touch the high ceiling in their old Victorian house. We often got to help; but some years, especially if we arrived just before Christmas, the tree would already be up, but we'd still help decorate it.

One year, just two days before Christmas, we arrived and the tree wasn't up. I asked Grandpa if we were going out to the woods to get one. He just smiled his little half smile, blue eyes twinkling mischievously, and said we weren't going out to the woods this year. I worried and watched my grandpa all afternoon, wondering what we were going to do about the tree, but he just went about his business as if nothing whatsoever was unusual. Finally just after dinner, Grandpa went and got his ax. At last, I thought, we *are* going to cut down a tree. But in the dark?

Grandpa grinned and told me to come outside. I followed him, wondering where he could cut a tree down at night. My grandparents' large home was situated on a small lot in the middle of town, with no U-cut trees anywhere nearby. But Grandpa went out to the parking strip next to their house and began whacking away at the trunk of one of his own mature holly trees—the tallest one, a beautiful tree loaded with bright red berries. I stared at him, in silent shock. What in the world was he doing? And what would Grandma say?

"The city says I gotta cut these trees down," he explained between whacks. "They're too close to the street. I figure if I take one out each Christmas, it will keep us in trees for three years." He grinned down at me, and the tree fell. Then my sister and I helped him carry it into the house, getting poked and pricked with every step of the way. I still wasn't sure what I thought about having a holly tree for a Christmas tree. I'd never heard of such a thing.

But when we had the tree in the stand and situated in its place of honor in one of the big bay windows, I knew that it was not a mistake. It was absolutely gorgeous. We all just stood and stared at its dark green glossy leaves and abundant bright red berries. "It's so beautiful," said Grandma. "It doesn't even need decorations." But my sister and I loved the process of decorating, and insisted it did. We began to hang lights and ornaments—carefully. It isn't easy decorating a holly tree. But with each new poke we laughed and complained good-naturedly.

For three years we had holly trees for Christmas. And now, whenever I get pricked by holly, I think of Grandpa. Later on in life, after my grandpa passed away, I learned about the symbolism of holly and why we use it at Christmas—and how the red berries represent droplets of Christ's blood. I don't know if my grandpa knew about all that, but he did know how to be a father to the fatherless. And he knew how to salvage good from evil. My grandpa didn't like to waste anything.

A FOUR-YEAR-OLD'S PRAYERS

A mother was listening to her four-year-old's prayers.
The little girl softly went through all the "God bless yous."
Then in a very loud voice asked for a brand new red bike
for her birthday. "God isn't deaf, dear," the mother said.
"I know! But Grandma's way out in the living room and she's
the one who's giving me the bike."

Author unknown

The Gift That Kept on Giving

Arleta Richardson
from Christmas Stories from Grandma's Attic

I was searching through Grandma's old trunk for some pictures when I came across a small, leather-bound book, the edges crumbly and dusty. It was a copy of Snowbound, and "John Greenleaf Whittier" was inscribed on the first page.

"Look, Grandma," I said. "Is this the book you told me about that Sarah Jane signed?"

"No," Grandma replied. She turned the book over lovingly. "This is the original one."

"But you sold that one to Warren Carter."

"I did," Grandma nodded. "The money he gave me helped get a coat with a fur collar for Ma's Christmas."

"But, how—?"

"How does it happen to be here? That's quite a story," Grandma said. "I guess I've never told you more than the first part of it."

"Tell me now," I urged her, and together we went back in time to Mabel's high school years.

Warren Carter did give me five dollars for my autographed copy of Snowbound, and for four years I was content with the copy that Sarah Jane had signed to look like the original. Ma enjoyed her coat so much that I never regretted the choice I had made.

Just before we graduated from high school, Warren stopped in to see me one evening.

"Mabel," he said, "you've given me a run for my money ever since we started school together. I probably never would have studied so hard if you had been easier to beat. I think you deserve a graduation gift for making me work."

He handed me a wrapped and ribboned package, and grinned happily as I opened it. It was the copy of *Snowbound* I had sold to him in the eighth grade. "Oh, Warren! Are you sure you want me to have this back?"

He nodded. "It's too valuable a thing for you ever to have sold. You've been a good friend over the years, and I want you to keep it."

The book went with me to my new home, and whenever I looked at it I thought of Warren's generosity. Then one Christmas, when Alma was about eight years old, there was no money for gifts for the family. Sarah Jane and I made doll clothes from scraps for our daughters' dolls.

"What are you doing for Len this year?" Sarah Jane asked as we worked on our sewing. "You haven't said anything about it."

"I've made him a sweater and socks," I said, "but the truth is, I want to get him a Bible. We have a nice family Bible, and the church Bible, of course, but he needs a reading Bible the size of his hymnal. I could get one from the catalog for seventy-five cents, but it's bound in cloth. The one I really have my eye on is bound in French Morocco and has gold edges."

"How much is it?"

"$1.40. I pick it up and look at it every time I go into Gages' store. Maybe I'll give it so much wear that they'll lower the price."

"Dorcas would let you get it and pay a little at a time," Sarah Jane said. "In fact, she would insist, if she knew you wanted it."

I shook my head. "Len wouldn't enjoy reading it if he knew I'd gone into debt for it. He would say that a Bible here and one at the church is enough. But I know how much he'd like one he could carry with him."

"How much do you still need?"

"Seventy-five cents."

"More than you'll get for your eggs," Sarah Jane said. "What else could you sell?"

"Nothing that I know of." I shrugged. I thought for a moment. "Well, maybe there is. My autographed copy of *Snowbound*."

Sarah Jane was appalled. "Oh, Mabel, no! I was thinking of something to eat, like cream or vegetables. That book is priceless!"

"So is Len," I replied. "I'll take it in to Dorcas and see if she'll buy it. Or at least trade it for the Bible."

Sarah Jane wasn't convinced that this was a good idea, but she said no more. The next time I went into town, I took the slender volume and explained my plan to Dorcas Gage.

"Are you sure, Mabel?" she protested. "This book is a treasure. Mr. Whittier is dead now, and there may not be many autographed copies of one of his most famous poems."

"I know. But how often do I read it? Len would read his Bible every day."

Dorcas was reluctant, but she took the book in return for the Bible, and I hurried home, more than pleased with my bargain.

When gifts were opened on Christmas morning, Len was delighted, as I knew he would be. As usual, we shared the day with Thomas and Sarah Jane. As we prepared to leave their home that evening, Sarah Jane handed me a small package.

"One more little gift," she said.

When I opened the present, I very nearly burst into tears. It was my autographed copy of *Snowbound*.

"Who knows what that book might buy next year?" Sarah Jane said with a grin. "I figured this was the best investment you could ever have."

But she was mistaken. Actually, the best investment of my life had been her friendship.

My Baby-Sitter, Mrs. H.

Charlotte Hale

Mrs. H., my baby-sitter, is as reliable as they come— even at the last moment, or on Saturdays, when I sometimes desperately need her help. Still...there are several nagging problems.

My mother, fair but strict, ran a tight ship. Sometimes when Mrs. H. watches Buddy, as she calls him, she lets him total phone numbers on the adding machine until the tape curls around the office chair. Or she lets him fill a sheet of paper with staples, or write a letter to himself, cover the envelope with stamps, then persuade the poor woman to walk with him to the nearest mailbox so he can drop his "letter" in.

Then there's food. Mother, a member of the Diet Police, permitted her children little or no food foolishness. Mrs. H., however, lets Buddy have vegetable soup or a hot dog for breakfast. When she bakes she slips him a handful of chocolate chips.

My own mother often read poetry and the children's classics to me. Mrs. H. also reads aloud, but lets my son choose what he'd like to hear. At times she reads automobile advertisements, tractor, motor oil or battery ads, until her voice gives out.

I'm not used to such indulgence. Is this sort of thing bad for the child? Mrs. H. disagrees. "He's a highly intelligent, sensitive boy. He's no trouble at all, and a perfect little gentleman," she asserts.

Still, with nobody else but my mother to compare her to, Mrs. H. confuses me. By now, of course, you've surely guessed my dilemma: the wonderful Mrs. H. and my own wonderful mother are one and the same person.

Believe me, though, they are nothing alike!

Stitches in Time

Philip Gulley
from Hometown Tales

E lectricity was discovered by the ancient Greeks, though it didn't find its way to my in-laws' farm until the summer of 1948. That's when the truck from the Orange County Rural Electric Cooperative made its way down Grimes Lake Road, planting poles and stringing wire. My mother-in-law, Ruby, sat on her front porch snapping beans while the linemen set the poles. That night she asked her husband, Howard, what he thought of her getting an electric sewing machine. Her treadle sewing machine was broken, the victim of two high-spirited boys who had pumped the treadle to an early death.

They drove to Bedford the next day to the Singer Sewing Center and bought a brand-new electric Singer with a buttonholer, a cabinet, and a chair. It cost two hundred and forty dollars, money they'd earned from selling a truckload of hogs to the meatpacking plant in New Solsberry.

Ruby set in to sewing for her boys. They added three children to their flock. More sewing. After supper, when the table was cleared and dishes washed, Ruby would bend over the machine, churning out clothes for her children and her neighbors. Thousands of dresses and shirts and pants. Clothes for dolls. Clothes for the minister's wife in town. Prom dresses. Wedding dresses. The Singer raised its needle millions of times. Her family would fall asleep under Ruby-made quilts, lulled to sleep by the Singer hum.

The kids grew up and moved away. Grandchildren came, eight in all. The Singer stitched maternity clothes, baby dresses, baptismal gowns, and quilts for the cribs. In 1987, Ruby called us on the phone, discouraged. After thirty-nine years, her Singer was limping. She took it to Mr. Gardner in the next town over. He fixed sewing machines but couldn't revive hers. He sent it away to Chicago. A month later it came back, a paper tag hanging from its cord. *Obsolete. Parts not available,* the tag read.

I went to a sewing machine store the next day to buy a new one. Her old one was metal. The new machines are plastic and have computers and cost the same as Ruby's first car. They give classes on how to use them. In the display window was a 1948 metal Singer blackhead.

"Does that one work?" I asked the man.

"I don't know," he said. "Let's plug it in." He plugged it in. It hummed to life.

"It's not for sale," he told me. "It's a display. There aren't a lot of these old Singer blackheads around anymore."

I told him about Ruby—how she lives by herself and sews to keep busy, how she only charges six dollars to make a dress because the people she sews for don't have a lot of money, how a lot of times she doesn't charge a dime, how sewing is her ministry.

He sold the machine to me for twenty-five dollars.

The next weekend we hauled it down to Ruby's. She was sitting on the front porch, watching for our car to round the corner on the gravel lane. She came outside and stood by the car as we opened the trunk. As she peered down at the '48 blackhead, a smile creased her face.

"It's just like my old one," she whispered.

We wrestled it inside and installed it in her old cabinet. Perfect fit. Plugged it in. When Ruby heard the hum, she clapped her hands.

It's still going strong. Ruby still charges six dollars a dress—unless it's a bride's dress; then she sews it by hand. That'll cost you fifteen dollars, but only if you can afford it.

Ruby travels north to visit her granddaughter Rachael. Rachael shows Ruby her Barbie doll, then asks Ruby if she could maybe please sew some clothes for Barbie. The first night Ruby is home, she bends over her '48 blackhead, stitching matching dresses for Rachael and her Barbie. Way past midnight she sews. The next morning she drives to town and mails a package northward. Three days later the phone rings. It's Rachael calling to say "Thank you" and "I love you" and "When can I see you again?"

On two other occasions, my wife and I found 1948 Singer blackheads in antique stores. We bought them and gave them to Ruby. She's got a lot of sewing ahead, and we don't want her to run out of sewing machines before she runs out of things to sew.

I don't always applaud every new thing that comes down the road, though I'm grateful that in 1948 electricity made its way down Grimes Lake Road. I'm grateful, too, for a woman who sews way into the night, who dispenses love one stitch at a time.

If we had known grandkids were so much fun,
we'd have had them first.

from a bumper sticker

I Love You, Grandpa!

Clare DeLong

S ome years ago my husband Wally and I decided that we would like to invite his father to come and live with us. The boys were both young—Brian, eleven, and Jeffrey, three. We thought they would benefit from his stay. Grandpa Marshall accepted our invitation, and that following September we traveled to upstate New York to bring him home. There were adjustments to be made from the beginning. Some were easy, some were not, but because of the love that existed between us, we seemed to muddle through.

One special thing we have always done every night was to tell each other that we loved each other. Our big old farm house would ring with "Good night, I love you," from one person to the next, each taking their turn. We happily added Grandpa Marshall to our list. In the beginning it must have seemed strange for him. For some reason those words were so very hard for him to say. He would tell each of us good night, but stopped there.

With Brian in school all day, Jeff and Grandpa Marshall were soon devoting much of their time to one another. A close relationship began to grow. I can remember walking into the living room one day to find Grandpa sitting quietly in his rocking chair—upon closer inspection I found out why. Jeff had him tied up, sitting at his feet with a grin on his face saying, "Look, Mom, we are playing cowboys and Indians."

I will never forget the night that became more special than any other. As usual we were saying our good nights, Brian and Jeffrey were climbing the stairs, each telling Grandpa "I love you," until finally disappearing around the turn, only to peek back to say it again one final time. It was then that I heard those words ring out as clear as a bell. It was Grandpa, he answered back not only good night but had added "I love you, too." My heart skipped a beat; it was those two boys, Brian and Jeff, who had touched his heart with love and, he had responded. From that moment on, Grandpa never seemed to mind saying those words. We could tell it became easier for him with the passing of time.

Wally's father lived with us for about a year. In that time we all developed a closeness with a very dear man. As I look back, I smile and am so grateful for us having had the chance to get to know him better during this special year of his life. When he returned to New York all of our visits and phone calls ended with those three words.

Grandpa Marshall died at 4:30 on a Sunday morning. As Wally held his hand, his final words to his son were, "I love you."

Faith

MOTHER'S COVERS

When you were small
And just a touch away,
I covered you with blankets
Against the cool night air.

But now that you are tall
And out of reach,
I fold my hands
And cover you in prayer.

Author unknown

Innocent Petitions

Robin Jones Gunn
from Mothering by Heart

When we lived in Reno, Rachel had a best friend named Kristin. We moved to Portland only a few days before Rachel's first day of second grade. Each night we talked about her new school and prayed together before she went to bed. The night before school started Rachel prayed that Jesus would give her a new best friend at this school and that her name would be Kristin. I felt compelled to alter her prayer but decided to let it go. How do I tell my child she shouldn't be so specific with God?

The next morning Rachel stood in front of the mirror while I combed her hair. She seemed lost in thought, and then suddenly she announced to me that Jesus was going to give her a new best friend. Her name would be Kristin, and she would have brown hair, just like the Kristin in Reno.

I quickly ran though all my mental notes on prayer. What would be the best way to explain to this child that prayer is not telling God what we have in mind for Him to do, but rather seeking His mind? I tried a few flimsy sentences. All fell flat. She seemed undaunted. I drove her to school still unable to find a way to protect her from her own prayer. I was afraid she would experience a spiritual crisis when she arrived at school and found no brunette Kristin in her class. What would that do to her innocent faith?

We entered the classroom, and Rachel found her name on her new desk. She lifted the top and began to examine the contents. I sat down at the desk next to hers and decided this would be a good time to explain how praying isn't like wishing. It's not magic. You can't ask God for something and expect it to materialize at your command. She needed to be willing to accept whatever new friends God brought to her.

I was about to plunge in, when out of the corner of my eye I noticed the name of the student who would occupy the desk next to Rachel. There, in bold black letters, was printed Kristin.

I could barely speak. "Rachel," I finally managed in a whisper, "look! There *is* a Kristin in your class. And she's going to sit right next to you!"

"I know, Mom. She's the one I prayed for."

The bell rang, and I practically staggered to the back of the classroom as the students began to come in. Rachel sat up straight, folded her hands on her desk, and grinned confidently.

I glued my eyes to that door. Four boys entered. Then a girl with blonde hair who took a seat in the first row. Two more boys and then, there she was! She sauntered shyly to the "Kristin" desk, caught Rachel's welcoming grin, and returned the same.

I probably don't need to mention that she had brown hair—down to her waist.

Or, that everything I really needed to know about prayer I learned in second grade.

The Operation

Dr. Norman Vincent Peale

H aving lunch with a group of people, I fell to talking with a surgeon, a very interesting man. "Doctor," I asked, "what was the greatest operation you ever performed?"

"Well," he said, "I really don't know. Many operations I have performed required all my skills. But perhaps the one that meant the most to me was the time I operated on a little girl who was given only a ten percent chance of survival. She was such a sweet little thing, and so pale when they brought her into the operating room.

"At that time, I was having a great deal of trouble, myself. I had a son who was a real problem and there were other things as well. I had allowed myself to become an unhappy man. As the nurses were preparing to administer the anesthetic to this little girl, she asked, 'Doctor, may I say something?'

"'Yes, honey,' I replied. 'What is it?'

"'Well,' she said, 'every night when I go to bed I say my prayers, and I'd like to say a prayer now.'

"'That's all right, honey, please say your prayer, and think of me, too, won't you?'

"In a sweet voice she prayed,

Jesus, tender Shepherd, hear me,
Bless thy little lamb tonight;
Through the darkness be thou near me:
Keep me safe till morning light.

"'And, dear God, please bless the doctor.' Then she added brightly, 'I'm ready now. And I'm not afraid, because Jesus loves me and He is right here with me and is going to bring me through okay.'

"I was blinded by tears," confessed the surgeon. "I had to turn away and occupy myself with another washup before I could start the operation. And I said, 'Dear God, if You never help me save another human being, help me save this little girl.' I operated on her and the miracle happened. She lived! Leaving the hospital that day, I realized that I was the one who had been operated on, not the girl. She taught me that if I take all my problems and put them in the hands of Jesus, He will see me through."

A SMALL BOY'S PRAYER

One night, when my son was small, I was saying prayers with him. The next day I was due to fly abroad to address an international law conference, and I was quite nervous.

I've prayed many prayers for him, but this time asked him to pray for me. This is what he said: "Dear Lord, please help my dad to be brave, and not to make too many mistakes." It's not a bad prayer for every father.

Rob Parsons
from Sixty Minute Father

A Bit of Eternity

Author unknown

Some years ago in England there was a postal clerk—old postal clerk #34. He had drawn the short-straw that year and so he had to hold the position of what they called the "nixie" clerk...the guy who had to dead-end all of the Christmas letters addressed to Santa Claus at the North Pole. And so he was doing his Grinch kind of job. In the middle of it, he came across an envelope that he recognized because the return address was his own...302 Walnut...and he recognized the handwriting of his little daughter, Miriam. So he decided he would open that one rather than just nix it, and he read in his daughter's handwriting these words:

Dear Santa Claus,

We are very sad at our home this year, and I don't want you to bring me anything. Little Charlie, my brother went up to heaven last week and all I want you to do when you come to my house is take his toys to him. I'll leave them in the corner by the chimney—his hobbyhorse, his train, and everything. You see he'll be lost in heaven without them...especially without his horse. He loved riding that horse so much. So you just take them to him and you needn't mind leaving me anything. If you could, though, if you could, give Daddy something that will make him stop crying all the time. It would be the best thing you could do for me if you could give him something that would make him stop crying. I heard him tell Mommy, that only eternity could cure him. Could you give him some of that?

Jump

Walter Wangerin Jr.
from Mourning into Dancing

When I was a boy...I told people that my father was stronger than anyone else in the world...

So I would go out on the front porch and roar to the neighborhood: "My daddy's arm is as strong as a truck! The strongest man in the world...."

In those days a cherry tree grew in our backyard. This was my hiding place. Ten feet above the ground a stout limb made a horizontal fork, a cradle on which I could lie face down, reading, thinking, being alone. Nobody bothered me there. Even my parents didn't know where I went to hide. Sometimes Daddy would come out and call, "Wally? Wally?" but he didn't see me in the leaves.

I felt very tricky.

Then came the thunderstorm....

One day suddenly, a wind tore through the backyard and struck my cherry tree with such force that it ripped the book from my hands and nearly threw me from the limb. I locked my arms around the forking branches and hung on. My head hung down between them. I tried to wind my legs around the limb, but the whole tree was wallowing in the wind....

"Daddeeeeeeee!"

There he was.... The branches swept up and down, like huge waves on an ocean—and Daddy saw me, and right away he came out into the wind and the weather, and I felt so relieved because I just took it for granted that he would climb right up the tree to get me.

But that wasn't his plan at all.

He came to a spot right below me and lifted his arms and shouted, "Jump."

"What?"

"Jump. I'll catch you."

Jump? I had a crazy man for a father. He was standing six or seven miles beneath me, holding up two skinny arms and telling me to jump. If I jumped, he'd miss. I'd hit the ground and die....

But the wind and the rain slapped that cherry tree, bent it back, and cracked my limb at the trunk. I dropped a foot. My eyes flew open. Then the wood whined and splintered and sank, and so did I, in bloody terror.

No, I did not jump. I let go. I surrendered.

I fell.

In a fast, eternal moment I despaired and plummeted. *This, I thought, is what it's like to die—*

But my father caught me....

Now, in such a storm the tree which was our stable world is shaken, and instinct makes us grab it tighter: by our own strength we grip the habits that have helped us in the past, repeating them, believing them. We'd rather trust what *is* than what *might be*: that is, our power, our reason and feeling and endurance...We spend a long time screaming *No!*...

But always, God is present. God has always been present. And it is God who says, "Jump."

Learned by Heart

Tim Hansel
from You Gotta Keep Dancin'

The Lord is my shepherd, I shall not want...
PSALM 23:1, KJV

I n his beautiful book, *I Shall Not Want*, Robert Ketchum tells of a Sunday school teacher who asked her group of children if anyone could quote the entire Twenty-third Psalm. A golden-haired four-and-a-half-year-old girl was among those who raised their hands. A bit skeptical, the teacher asked if she could really quote the entire psalm. The little girl came to the rostrum, faced the class, made a perky little bow, and said: "The Lord is my shepherd, *that's all I want.*" She bowed again and went and sat down. That may well be the greatest interpretation I've ever heard.

She Went Over Her Daddy's Head

Otto Whittaker

I t's been fifteen years since I heard this little story. You may find it as unforgettable as I did.

In the southern states that summer, the mercury had hung in or near the 90s for five or six straight weeks. It was on a morning when the sun was blazing that the testifier told us.

Just a few days before, his five-year-old daughter had come to him with a little note of anguish in her voice. She had told him, "Daddy, it's still awful hot," and asked, "can we go swimming?"

"I had to tell her no," her daddy reported. "It costs about eight dollars to take my family swimming, so we don't go very often. 'Some other time,' I told her.

"But that wasn't enough. She wanted to know 'Why not now?' So I explained that we just didn't have the money for it."

Well, to the little girl that was a good explanation but a poor solution. She promptly took the matter to a Higher Court. "I'm going to ask God," she said.

And then, with just a tiny pinch of defiance, off she rushed to her bedroom.

Intrigued, her daddy followed on tiptoe and stood just outside her door, carefully out of sight, to hear what she would ask of God. And this is what he heard:

"God, it's awful hot down here today, just awful hot. And I want to go swimming. But they charge a lot of money, and my daddy can't take us because he hasn't got that much. So will you please do something? Thank you, God. Amen."

Oh, the love in that father's voice when he told what the little girl did next: She put on her bathing suit. Then she got a towel. And then, towel draped around her neck, she headed for the front porch, announcing as she went that she was going outside to wait for God to do something.

She'd just taken her seat on the porch steps, elbows on knees and chin in hand, when the telephone rang. Her mother answered it.

The caller was the wife in a couple they knew, but did not know well. They were interesting and likable acquaintances, but not yet close friends.

"We've been wanting to know you folks better," she told the little girl's mother. "Today's another scorcher, and we wondered whether you'd like to come over to the club with us for some swimming?"

"Oh, we'd love to!" the mother replied. "But how soon are you going? I've been lazy this morning, and there are a few things I have to do before…"

"Oh, no problem!" the caller said. "We're not ready yet either. I didn't even think of it until a few minutes ago."

Covered with Prayer

Linda Vogel

My precious one,

In celebration of your arrival I've made you a special gift, called a prayer blanket. When you are covered with it, know that you are covered in prayer. Each tiny stitch represents a prayer prayed for you. Here are my ten prayers for you:

1. Like a ball of yarn that turns into a beautiful blanket, God has a beautiful plan for your life.

I pray you discover it (Jeremiah 1:5).

2. This blanket is made with my human hands. But you are "fearfully and wonderfully made" by divine hands.

I pray you will know how special you are to God (Psalm 139:14).

3. If I miss a stitch, the blanket will unravel. God has wonderful plans for every step of your life.

I pray you will look to Him for His plan and know that even when we as your family miss a stitch or make a mistake, God can redeem that as we trust Him (Proverbs 28:13).

4. If I go back and correct a stitch, the blanket won't be "holey." If you go back and confess your sins, your life will be holy.

I pray you will have the courage to confess wrongdoing so you can live a holy life (1 John 1:9).

5. This blanket has many stitches, but they are nothing compared to the number of thoughts God has toward you.

I pray you will think about God and know He thinks about you (Psalm 139:17).

6. It took three strands wrapped together to make a strong yarn for this blanket. It will take three parts (you, your family, and God) to make a strong life for you. And it will take three divine parts of God to keep you together.

I pray you will depend on God and your family (Ecclesiastes 4:12).

7. The border on this blanket protects the blanket from becoming misshapen. God wants to put a border around your life to keep you safe from harm.

I pray you will stay within the borders God sets for you (Job 1:10).

8. My hope for this prayer blanket is to keep you warm and secure. How much more is God's plan! He wants to give you a "future and hope."

I pray you will always put your hope in God (Jeremiah 29:11).

9. When you are covered by this blanket, know you are covered in love and prayer. God wants to also cover you with the love of His Son.

I pray you will come to love Jesus at an early age (John 14:21).

10. Although you will outgrow this blanket,

I pray you will never want to outgrow your need for God (1 John 4:1–17).

Love,
Your grandmother

The Perfect Spring Day

Sandy Snavely

I t was the perfect spring day—the kind that frees the imaginations of little boys and sends them off into uncertain worlds of adventure. On one such day our son Dean stood in the backyard, feeling the breeze blowing through his hair and decided it was time to give his kite its first flight of the season.

It wasn't long before I heard a muffled sound that troubled my mother's heart. I followed the noise until it led me to our deck in the backyard. There, I found Dean huddled at the top of the stairs, fumbling with a large wad of tangled fishing line while tears drizzled down his chubby little cheeks.

Dean was a child who attracted knots. He had knots in his hair, knots in his shoelaces, knots in his yo-yo strings and knots in anything else that could possibly end up knotted.

I scooted down next to our son, who looked up at me with all the loyalty of a basset hound, as he handed me his ball of knots. Since the time he was a toddler I had come to cherish his confidence in my ability to be his problem solver. While I went to work, toiling over the untamable mess, we chatted about why fishing line was used for fishing and kite string was used for flying kites. I held in my hands the knot that wouldn't be unknotted—and I knew my inability to fix this particular problem was about to break my child's trusting heart.

Dean and I both learned a valuable lesson that morning. There are times when problems appear as knots in our lives, but there are times when our lives *are* the problem, with tangles too big for human hands to undo. Little boys and their mothers need the assurance that we can run to Someone greater than ourselves when our dreams have been shattered by the illusive imaginations of spring.

There's Robby!

Ruth Bell Graham
from Legacy of a Pack Rat

The room was quiet and semidarkened. The elderly lady lying against the pillow listened as her son, Robert, talked of the family, her friends, and other things of interest to her.

She looked forward to his daily visits. Madison, where he lived, was not far from Nashville, and Robert spent as much time as he could with his mother, knowing, as ill as she was, each visit might be his last. As he talked, his eyes took in every detail of her loved face, every line—and there were more lines than curves now—the white hair, the tired, still loving eyes. When time came to leave, he kissed her gently on her forehead, assuring her he would be back the next day.

Arriving back at his home in Madison, he found Robin, his seventeen-year-old, was ill with a strange fever.

The next few days his time was completely taken up between his son and his mother.

He did not tell his mother of Robin's illness. He was her oldest grandson—the pride and joy of her life.

Then, suddenly, Robin was gone. His death shocked the whole community as well as his family. The whole thing had happened so quickly. And seventeen is too young to die.

As soon as the funeral was over, Mr. Armistead hurried to his mother's bedside, praying nothing in his manner would betray the fact he had just buried his firstborn. It would be more than his mother could take in her condition.

The doctor was in the room as he entered. His mother was lying with her eyes closed.

"She is in a coma," the doctor said gently. He knew something of the strain this man had been under, his faithful visits to his mother, the death of his son, the funeral from which he had just come…

The doctor put his hand on Mr. Armistead's shoulder in wordless sympathy.

"Just sit beside her," he said, "she might come to.…" And he left them together.

Mr. Armistead's heart was heavy as he sat in the gathering twilight.

He lit the lamp on the bedside table, and the shadows receded.

Soon she opened her eyes, and smiling in recognition, she put her hand on her son's knee.

"Bob…," she said his name lovingly—and drifted into a coma again.

Quietly Mr. Armistead sat on, his hand over hers, his eyes never leaving her face. After awhile there was a slight movement on the pillow.

His mother's eyes were open and there was a far-off look in them, as if she were seeing beyond the room. A look of wonder passed over her face.

"I see Jesus," she exclaimed, adding, "why there's Father…and there's Mother…"

And then,

"And there's Robby! I didn't know Robby had died.…"

Her hand patted her son's knee gently.

"Poor Bob…," she said softly, and was gone.

Thoughts Midstream

Joni Eareckson Tada
from Glorious Intruder

When I was little and went horseback riding with my sisters, I had a hard time keeping up. My problem was that I was riding a little pony only half the size of their mounts. I had to gallop twice as fast just to keep up.

I didn't mind. I took it as a challenge—until we came to the edge of a river. My sisters on their big horses thought it was fun and exciting to cross the river at the deepest part. They never seemed to notice that my little pony sank quite a bit deeper into the swirling waters. It was scary, but I wasn't about to let them know.

One crossing in particular sticks in my memory: the Gorsuch Switch Crossing on the Patapsco River. It had rained earlier that week and the river was brown and swollen. As our horses waded out toward midstream, I became transfixed staring at the swirling waters rushing around the legs of my pony. It made me scared and dizzy. I began to lose my balance in the saddle.

The voice of my sister Jay finally broke through my panic.

"Look up, Joni! Keep looking up!"

Sure enough, as soon as I focused on my sister on the other side, I was able to regain my balance and finish the crossing.

That little story came to mind recently when I was reading about Peter in Matthew 14. It seems he had a similar problem as he walked on the water toward the Lord Jesus. He looked down at the raging waters, got dizzy, and lost his balance. Because he took his eyes off the Lord and put them on the swirling waves around him, he began to sink.

How much we are like him! Instead of resting on the Word

of God, we let our circumstances almost transfix us, absorbing us to the point where we begin to lose our spiritual equilibrium. We become dizzy with fear and anxiety. And before you know it, we've lost all balance.

It's easy to panic, isn't it? And admittedly, it's hard to look up—especially when you feel like you're sinking.

But my pony and I made it across the Patapsco and Peter made it back to his boat. Thousands before you, enduring the gale force winds of circumstance, have made it through, keeping their eyes on the Lord Jesus. How about you?

If you can't find a way out, try looking up!

As for me and my household,
We will serve the Lord.
Joshua 24:15

I Am a Mother's Prayer

Author unknown

I am a mother's prayer. I am sometimes clothed in beautiful language that has been stitched together with the needles of love in the quiet chambers of the heart, and sometimes I am arrayed only in the halting phrases interrupted by tears which have been torn like living roots from the deep soil of human emotion. I am a frequent watcher of the night. I have often seen the dawn break over the hills and flood the valleys with light and the dew of the gardens has been shaken from my eyes as I waited and cried at the gates of God.

I am a mother's prayer: there is no language I cannot speak; and no barrier of race or color causes my feet to stumble. I am born before the child is born, and ere the day of deliverance comes, I have often stood at the altar of the Lord with the gift of an unborn life in my hands, blending my joyful and tearful voice with the prayers and tears of the father. I have rushed ahead of the nurse through the corridors of the hospital praying that the babe would be perfect, and I have sat dumb and mute in the presence of delight over a tiny bit of humanity, so overwhelmed I have been able to do nothing but strike my fingers on the harps of gratitude and say, "Well, thank the Lord!"

I am a mother's prayer: I have watched over the cradle; I have sustained a whole household while we waited for a doctor to come. I have mixed medicine and held up a thermometer that read 104°. I have sighed with relief over the sweat in the little one's curls because the crisis was past. I have stood by a graveside and picked a few flowers to take home like old memories, and cast my arms around the promises of God to just hang on and wait until I could feel underneath me the everlasting arms.

I am a mother's prayer: I have walked and knelt in every room of the house; I have fondled the old Book, sat quietly at the kitchen table, and been hurled around the world to follow a boy who went to war. I have sought through hospitals and army camps and battlefield. I have dogged the steps of sons and daughters in college and university, in the big city looking for a job. I have been in strange places, for I have even gone down into honky-tonks and dens of sin, into night clubs and saloons and back alleys and along dark streets. I have ridden in automobiles and planes and ships seeking and sheltering and guiding and reminding and tugging and pulling toward home and Heaven.

I am a mother's prayer: I have filled pantries with provision when the earthly provided was gone. I have sung songs in the night when there was nothing to sing about but the faithfulness of God. I have been pressed so close to the promises of the Word that the imprint of their truth is fragrant about me. I have lingered on the lips of the dying like a trembling melody echoed from Heaven.

I am a mother's prayer: I am not unanswered, although mother may be gone, although the home may be dissolved into dust, although the little marker in the graveyard grows dim. I am still here: and as long as God is God, and truth is truth, and the promises of God are "yes and amen," I will continue to woo and win and strive and plead with boys and girls whose mothers are in Glory, but whose ambassador I have been appointed by the King Emmanuel. I am a mother's prayer....

I'll Be Back Soon

Luis Palau
from God is Relevant

S hortly after the start of World War II, a soldier told his wife "I'll be back soon," then left her and their infant son to head into combat.

Five years went by. The young mother would show her boy a portrait of the soldier and say, "See, that's your daddy. One day he's going to come home." In reality, she didn't know what to expect.

One morning the boy said, "Mommy, wouldn't it be great if Daddy would just step out of the picture frame?"

In a sense that's what God did two thousand years ago. As part of his eternal plan, he stepped out of heaven and became a man so you and I could look at Jesus and say, "That's what God looks like."

Reference Point

Max Lucado
from The Final Week of Jesus

One of the reference points of London is the Charing Cross. It is near the geographical center of the city and serves as a navigational tool for those confused by the streets.

A little girl was lost in the great city. A policeman found her. Between sobs and tears, she explained she didn't know her way home. He asked her if she knew her address. She didn't. He asked her phone number; she didn't know that either. But when he asked her what she knew, suddenly her face lit up.

"I know the Cross," she said. "Show me the Cross and I can find my way home from there."

Homeward Journey

Janet Paschal
from The Good Road

I t was a warm Saturday afternoon. A Carolina breeze was steadily moving through the long grass and the proud, full branches. I was driving home, back to the little corner of the world where I grew up. I was en route to a modest house on a corner lot bordered by pine trees, vegetable gardens and neighbors who still bake casseroles for each other.

I was thinking that when I arrive, my dad (most likely atop his newly painted tractor) will head across the freshly mown lawn. He'll hug me long and hard until the back door slams. My mom will reach for me, smiling, and announce, "I've a fresh pitcher of iced tea. Who's ready for a glass?" In a few moments my nephew will bound across the road, dog in tow.

I knew I'd spend the next few days with people who love me unconditionally. The number of records I sell doesn't matter to them. The awards I have or haven't received are insignificant. My career, whether rocketing or plummeting, is rarely mentioned. They just care that I come. They just want me.

What really matters is home. This is the stuff I am made of. This is what is important to me.

We are all on a homeward journey. God patiently plans our routes and polices our perils. He watches us maneuver through detours and treacherous places. He even sees us make an occasional wrong turn then keep going anyway.

But always He waits. Long ago He paved the way and marked the direction for us to come to Him. He prepared a place of rest that is beyond the reaches of our imaginations—a welcome center built by His own hand.

He doesn't care what religious label we bear. Our nationality or net worth won't matter. He just cares that we come. He just wants us home.

After my grandfather was diagnosed with Alzheimer's disease he had trouble recognizing people and places, like his home. He kept insisting that it was someone else's house, and he wasn't home yet.

I guess he was right.

Trust in the dark,
trust in the light,
trust at night
and trust in the morning,
and you will find that the faith
which may begin by mighty effort,
will end sooner or later
by becoming the easy
and natural habit of the soul.

Hannah Whitall Smith
from The Christian's Secret of a Happy Life

Come Home!

Billy Graham
from Unto the Hills

O nce there was a widow and her son who lived in a miserable attic. Years before, she had married against her parents' wishes and had gone with her husband to live in a foreign land.

He had proved irresponsible and unfaithful, and after a few years he died without having made any provision for her and the child. It was with the utmost difficulty that she managed to scrape together the bare necessities of life.

The happiest times in the child's life were those when the mother took him in her arms and told him about her father's house in the old country. She told him of the grassy lawn, the noble trees, the wild flowers, and the delicious meals.

The child had never seen his grandfather's home, but to him it was the most beautiful place in all the world....

One day the postman knocked at the attic door. The mother recognized the handwriting on the letter and with trembling fingers broke the seal. There was a check and a slip of paper with just two words: "Come Home."

Some day a similar experience will be ours—an experience shared by all who know Christ.... We do not know when the call will come. But some day a loving hand will be laid upon our shoulder and this brief message will be given: "Come Home."

All of us who know Christ personally need not be afraid to die. Death to the Christian is "going home."

First Words

Ruth Bell Graham
from Legacy of a Pack Rat

I shall miss Mother this Christmas," the clerk in the Asheville store told me. Her mother had died recently, and this would be the first Christmas without her.

"I used to go home in the evenings, and we'd have such good times together."

The day they put her in the hospital, the doctor told the children they would have to stay out of her room in order for her to rest and get adjusted.

"So I stayed out in the hall," she continued, "waiting...listening. Finally I could stand it no longer, and I went in.

"'I thought you'd never come!' Mother said."

Blinking back the tears, the clerk added, with a smile, "You know, I'm thinking they'll be the first words she'll say to me when I get to Heaven!"

Amazing Grace

Philip Yancey
from What's So Amazing about Grace?

Bill Moyers' documentary film on the hymn "Amazing Grace" includes a scene filmed in Wembley Stadium in London. Various musical groups, mostly rock bands, had gathered together in celebration of the changes in South Africa, and for some reason the promoters scheduled an opera singer, Jessye Norman, as the closing act.

The film cuts back and forth between scenes of the unruly crowd in the stadium and Jessye Norman being interviewed. For twelve hours groups like Guns 'n' Roses have blasted the crowd through banks of speakers, riling up fans already high on booze and dope. The crowd yells for more curtain calls, and the rock groups oblige. Meanwhile, Jessye Norman sits in her dressing room discussing "Amazing Grace" with Moyers.

Finally, the time comes for her to sing. A single circle of light follows Norman, a majestic African-American woman wearing a flowing African dashiki, as she strolls on stage. No backup band, no musical instruments, just Jessye. The crowd stirs, restless. Few recognize the opera diva. A voice yells for more Guns 'n' Roses. Others take up the cry. The scene is getting ugly.

Alone, *a capella*, Jessye Norman begins to sing, very slowly:

Amazing grace, how sweet the sound
    That saved a wretch like me!
I once was lost but now am found—
    Was blind, but now I see.

A remarkable thing happens in Wembley Stadium that night. Seventy thousand raucous fans fall silent before her aria of grace.

By the time Norman reaches the second verse, "'Twas grace that taught my heart to fear, And grace my fears relieved...," the soprano has the crowd in her hands.

By the time she reaches the third verse, "'Tis grace has brought me safe this far, And grace will lead me home," several thousand fans are singing along, digging far back in nearly lost memories for words they heard long ago.

> *When we've been there ten thousand years,*
> *Bright shining as the sun*
> *We've no less days to sing God's praise*
> *Than when we first begun.*

Jessye Norman later confessed she had no idea what power descended on Wembley Stadium that night. I think I know. The world thirsts for grace. When grace descends, the world falls silent before it.

Notes

TREASURE

*Richer than I you can never be
I had a mother who read to me.*

Strickland Gillilan

*This section includes a special message from Gloria Gaither
and recommendations for family reading.*

Honey for the Heart

Alice Gray

S ome of my best memories are of Mother reading or telling stories to my sisters and me. She delighted us with mischievous tales of Peter Rabbit, inspired us with dramatic recitations of "Oh Captain! My Captain!" by Walt Whitman, and sometimes sang melancholy story-songs like that of Red Wing, an Indian maiden whose sweetheart died in battle.

On Saturdays, as soon as our chores were finished, Mother sent my friend Maggie and me to the neighborhood library. We raced down the road on our bicycles, blonde braids flying in the wind, and checked out a stack of books. Then we'd hurry home, curl up on the couch and read the afternoon away, lost in faraway adventures.

Even as her health declined, Mother found stories and gave them to me. Sometimes she added a note in shaky handwriting as a reminder for me to share them with our two grown sons, Bob and James. Other times, she'd simply mark a tiny heart in the margin. The first book in the *Stories for the Heart* series included many of her favorites gathered through the years. But Mother did more than teach me to love stories; she inspired my imagination and built my moral character and faith. The tender memories and rich heritage she left are like honey for my heart.

I want to pass that heritage on and so have included this special section as a resource for good family books. Featured is a personal letter from Gloria Gaither sharing some of her family's traditions and favorite books. Next there are warm comments written by Christian leaders and authors about the importance of family reading. Finally, there is a treasured resource of interesting and fun books—all of which have good moral and spiritual values.

Enjoy the adventure as you make honey for your family's heart.

No Frigate Like a Book

Gloria Gaither

I am thankful to have grown up in a family where a great achievement was a well-written paragraph or an articulately communicated thought and whose idea of a wonderful evening was one spent sharing with each other nuggets from books we were reading. Our most valued possession was our library. On its shelves were my father's volumes of theology, mother's collection of poetry, prose and fiction, and my sister's and my books that traced our love of reading from nursery rhymes to *Hardy Boys* novels and, later, on to the classics of English and American literature: Hardy, Shakespeare, Milton, Wolfe, Steinbeck, Faulkner, Fitzgerald, Hawthorne, Hemingway, Austen.

My earliest memories seem to be of poetry and the principles of life that were hidden in the musical pattern of their words. My mother took every opportunity to discuss with us, for instance, the cycle of bad choices reflected in the nursery rhyme that sang:

I met a crooked man
Who walked a crooked mile
Who found a crooked sixpence
Upon a crooked stile;
He bought a crooked cat
Who caught a crooked mouse
And they all lived together
In a little crooked house.

Or the sad smallness of one who would waste great opportunity on the visionless habits of a lifetime:

"Pussycat, pussycat where have you been?"
"I've been to London to visit the Queen."
"Pussycat, pussycat what did you there?"
"I frightened the little mouse under the chair."

Oh well, as Mother used to say, "you can't make a silk purse out of a pig's ear." Only God can change a nature.

In story and poetry I met "The Village Blacksmith," the "headless horseman," and Ichabod Crane, sad Barbara Allen, Jack the Giant Killer and all the characters that would assail or encourage the Pilgrim's progress. I wept to sing of "Old Shep" and never did I walk through a meadow or field that I did not secretly search for "My Little Doll, Dears."

It was always made abundantly clear to me that the fictional characters of great poetry, folk songs, or stories were teaching the same truths that we found lived out in the real lives of the historical figures of the Bible. We actively looked for verses of Scripture that confirmed the universal principles: "what a man soweth, that shall he also reap," or "the paths of a good man are ordered by the Lord," or "the wicked are...like the chaff which the wind driveth away."

I have had the joy of sharing great literature with my children (all of whom are now writers and creators of music, art or poetry) and now my grandchildren. I find some of the most exciting books today are the books written for children, but with truths no adult should miss. And I am saddened by the current movement led by those who would keep our children from great literature for the purpose of "making" or "keeping" them Christian. I have come to believe more than ever what my parents practiced: it is always better to teach a child *how* to think than to tell them *what* to think; for we parents could never hope to cover all the "whats" of a changing world, but the child who can discern for herself is prepared for any world.

I would hope no child would grow up without being

exposed *with* his parents to these great old and current "classics."

Children's Garden of Verses by Robert Lewis Stevenson

All the Places to Love by Patricia MacLachlan

Hope for the Flowers by Trina Paulus

The Velveteen Rabbit by Marjery Williams

The Giving Tree, The Missing Piece, Where the Sidewalk Ends and *Light in the Attic* by Shel Silverstein (These last two will make the whole family laugh, and we should laugh at a lot more than we do.)

The Chronicles of Narnia by C. S. Lewis

The Austin Family series and the *Wrinkle in Time* series by Madeleine L'Engle

Anne of Green Gables series and the *Emily* series by L. M. Montgomery

Little Women by Louisa May Alcott

The Red Pony by John Steinbeck

Lassie Come Home by Eric Knight, Rosemary Wells

The Black Stallion by Walter Farley

Black Beauty by Robin McKinley

Tom Sawyer by Mark Twain

The Collected Words of James Whitcomb Riley (Have fun with the Midwest dialect!) by James Whitcomb Riley

"Stopping by the Woods on a Snowy Evening" by Robert Frost (This poem is in a beautiful children's edition published by Holt, Rinehart and Winston.)

"Swinger of Birches" by Robert Frost (Children's edition published by Stemmer House)

The Collected Stories of Leo Lionni by Leo Lionni

Alexander and the Horrible, No Good, Very Bad Day by Judith Viorst

William Gordon McDonald Partridge by Mem Fox

James and the Giant Peach by Roald Dahl

The Best Christmas Pageant Ever by Barbara Robinson

The best Bible story book I have ever found is still the accurate and complete *Egermeier Bible Story Book* by Elsie Egermeier, published by Warner Press. Use for the whole family and children of all ages. This one should be served up with breakfast and at bedtime for family nourishment of the soul.

No television program, no matter how good, can take the place of a family reading together, discussing great ideas, and applying the important principles to the daily events of life. Fortunate indeed is the child who is taught to fall in love with the truth and is given the power of words to express it in story, illustration, and song. The ancient mandate to parents found in the Bible still speaks to the modern home.

And thou shalt love the LORD thy God with all thine heart, and with all thy soul, and with all thy might.
And these words, which I command thee this day, shall be in thine heart:
And thou shalt teach them diligently unto thy children, and shalt talk of them when thou sittest in thine house, and when thou walkest by the way, and when thou liest down, and when thou risest up.
And thou shalt bind them for a sign upon thine hand, and they shall be as frontlets between thine eyes.
And thou shalt write them upon the posts of thy house, and on thy gates.

Deuteronomy 6:5–9, KJV

To become a part of our children's lives, great values must be illustrated not only in story, song and poetry, but also in daily walks in the park, transactions at the grocery store and the car-service garage. They must be spoken in prayer, at church, at school and especially at home. Our shared human journey is perhaps most of all about a God of history who reaches into the daily of our mundane lives with revelations and insight that lift us above our baser selves into the presence of angels. And sometimes those angels wear cowboy boots!

Editor's note: For a more extended biography of family reading, see the "recommended reading" list in the back of *Let's Make a Memory* and *Let's Hide the Word* by Gloria Gaither with Shirley Dobson, published by Word.

FROM OUR FAMILY TO YOURS

I was given a sixteen-book set as a child called *My Book House*, which had all the classic stories in it. I lived in that set of books, containing *The Little Engine That Could* and the like—I still have them.

James Dobson
Founder and President of Focus on the Family

One of our favorite resources is Ken Taylor's *The Bible in Pictures for Little Eyes*. Each chapter takes only a couple of minutes to read, and the questions at the end of each story encourage children to listen carefully. Kids love to see who can recall the answers first.

Luis and Pat Palau
from *How to Lead Your Child to Christ*

Our family's favorite holiday classic is *Little Lord Fauntleroy*.

Joseph M. Stowell
President of Moody Bible Institute

On vacation we took a duffel bag full of books—reading all we could. It was important for us to read aloud together as a family.

Colleen Townsend Evans
Author of *Teaching Your Child to Pray*

And then, there were Father's books. He couldn't get his hands on enough of them. When other girls my age were hearing fairy stories, I was listening to him read about great adventurers, pioneering people who changed the world: Livingstone, Nightingale, and Goforth, a missionary in China.

Ingrid Trobisch
from *Keeper of the Springs*

Besides all the warm memories, reading also opens up worlds for children, and reading classics to and with children forms a solid background for excellent language development and comprehension, appreciation for literature, and a wide vocabulary.

Cheri Fuller
Author of *When Mothers Pray*

Reading to children encourages them to read for themselves. It also offers a precious time to be with them, talking with them, answering questions, encouraging their imaginations. It is a time to open their minds to God and His creation, His promises, His purpose. Reading means time, a lap to sit on, hands to turn pages and a voice of love—gifts to a child that last a lifetime.

Francine Rivers
Author of *Redeeming Love*

My children loved Dr. Suess and I enjoyed the fun language. We all memorized *Green Eggs and Ham* and to this day when together we all burst into a fun recitation.

Florence Littauer
Founder of CLASS Speakers, Inc.

I believe that reading consistently to one's children is the single best activity one can do to stimulate their mental growth.

Linda Sattgast
Author of *The Rhyme Bible*

Some of my happiest times as a little girl were sitting in front of my mother as she read to us kids—a fire blazing in the heating stove.

Anna Hayford
Author and speaker
wife of Pastor Jack Hayford

Children seeing Mom and Dad enjoying books creates a love for reading and stimulates the imagination.

Marilyn McAuley
Author of the *Peek and Find* series

We made a practice of reading at the dinner table each evening all the way through high school. Mom would read a chapter a night, then read the first line of the next chapter and close the book.

Gary and Anne Marie Ezzo
Founders of Growing Families International

Our daughter's favorite book was *Treasure of the Snow* by Patricia St. John. Her grandmother gave it to her and read it to her—a special memory.

Ruth Myers
Author of *31 Days of Praise*

BOOKS TO READ TOGETHER

We are grateful to many authors who wrote and recommended books for family reading. Following are the titles mentioned

A Little Princess
  Frances Hodgson Burnett

A Tale of Two Cities
  Charles Dickens

A Time of Wonder
  Robert McCloskey

The Adventures of Tom Sawyer
  Mark Twain

Aesop's Fables
All Creatures Great and Small
  James Herriot

Angry Waters
  Walt Morey

The Beloved Intruder
  Eugenia Price

Charlotte's Web
  E. B. White

Christy
  Catherine Marshall

The Crippled Lamb
  Max Lucado

Good Night Moon
  Margaret Wise Brown

Hind's Feet on High Places
  Hannah Hurnard

Hurlburt Bible Stories
In Grandma's Attic
  Arleta Richardson

In His Steps
  Charles M. Sheldon

In His Steps (Children's Edition)
  Helen Haidle

The Incredible Journey
  Sheila Burnford

Just So Stories
  Rudyard Kipling

Kidnapped
  Robert Louis Stevenson

The *Little House* Series
  Laura Ingalls Wilder

The Little Prince
  Antoine de Saint-Exupery

McGee and Me Series
  Bill Myers

The Nancy Drew Detective Mysteries Series

Not My Will
Francena H. Arnold

Old Yeller
Fred Gipson

One Wintry Night
Ruth Bell Graham

The Parable of the Lily
Liz Curtis Higgs

The Pilgrim's Progress
John Bunyan

Pollyanna
Eleanor H. Porter

The Prince and the Pauper
Mark Twain

Rebecca of Sunnybrook Farm
Kate Douglas Wiggin

The Secret Garden
Frances Hodgson Burnett

Someday Heaven
Larry Libby

The Sugar Creek Gang Series
Paul Hutchens

The Tales of Peter Rabbit
Beatrix Potter

The Trumpet of the Swan
E. B. White

The Wind in the Willows
Kenneth Grahame

Winnie-the-Pooh
A. A. Milne

Editors note:

In 1997, the Family Research Council published a booklet called *Home Remedies*. It has sixteen pages of recommended books divided by age group and categories. The sixty-page booklet can be ordered by calling 1-800-225-4008. Recommended donation is $4.

In 1989 Gladys Hunt wrote *Honey for a Child's Heart* (Zondervan Publishing, Grand Rapids, MI). It is still available and is a popular and valuable resource about children's literature.

Bibliography

More than a thousand books were researched for this collection of stories as well as reviewing hundreds of stories sent by friends and readers of the *Stories for the Heart* series. Reasonable care has been taken to trace original ownership, and when necessary, obtain permission to reprint. If I have overlooked giving proper credit to anyone, please accept my apologies. If you will contact Multnomah Publishers, Inc., Post Office Box 1720, Sisters, Oregon 97759, corrections will be made prior to additional printings.

Notes and acknowledgments are listed by story title in the order they appear in each section of the book. For permission to reprint any of the stories please request permission from the original source listed in the following bibliography. Grateful acknowledgement is made to authors, publishers, and agents who granted permission for reprinting these stories.

COMPASSION

"Look Alikes" by Linda Mango. Reprinted with permission from the April 1994 *Reader's Digest*. © 1994 by the Reader's Digest Association, Inc.

"Ragamuffin Brother" by Ron Mehl from *God Works the Night Shift* (Multnomah Publishers, Inc., Sisters, OR), © 1994. Used by permission.

"Lessons in Baseball" by Chick Moorman from *Where the Heart Is: Stories of Home and Family* (Personal Power Press, Saginaw, MI), © 1996. Used by permission of the author.

"The Tree Man" by James W. H. Tumber from December 1995 *Highlights for Children* (Highlights for Children, Inc., Columbus, OH), © 1995. Used by permission.

"A Candle for Barbara" by Phyllis Reynolds Naylor from *Christmas through the Years* (Crest Books, Alexandria, VA), © 1997. © 1980 by Phyllis Reynolds Naylor. Used by permission.

"Uncle Bun" by Jan Nations, © 1997. Used by permission of the author.

"Gingham Aprons" by Dorothy Canfield Fisher, © Vivian Scott Hixon. Used by permission.

ENCOURAGEMENT

Kirkpatrick. Used by permission.

"Grandma's Garden" by Lynnette Curtis, © 1997. Used by permission of the author. Lynnette Curtis is a graduate student at the University of Nevada, Las Vegas and works as an editorial assistant at the Las Vegas *Review-Journal*. She may be reached by e-mail at MsNettiel@aol.com.

"Beauty Contest" by Allison Harms, freelance writer, Lake Oswego, OR, © 1997. Used by permission of the author.

"Sparky" by Earl Nightingale from *More of...The Best of Bits and Pieces*. Used by permission. Reprinted by permission of the Economics Press, Inc., Fairfield, N.J. 07004. 800-526-2554. Fax: 973-227-9742. E-mail: info@epinc.com. Website: http//www.epinc.com. (The Economics Press, Inc., Fairfield, NJ), © 1997.

"Perceptive?" by Gary Smalley from *Home Remedies*, by Gary Smalley and John Trent (Multnomah Publishers, Inc., Sisters, OR), © 1991. Used by permission.

"Twice Blessed" by Kathryn Lay, freelance writer of 300 inspirational and children's stories, who lives in Bedford, TX, © 1997. Used by permission of the author.

"Art 101" author unknown, quoted from *Chicken Soup for the Mother's Soul* (Health Communications, Inc., Deerfield Beach, FL).

"A Gift from My Dad" by Steve Dwinnells from *Decision* magazine, December 1997. (Billy Graham Evangelistic Association, Minneapolis, MN), © 1997 by Steve Dwinnells. Used by permission. All rights reserved.

"Mistaken Identity" by James Dobson from *Home with a Heart* (Tyndale House Publishers, Inc., Wheaton, IL), © 1996. Used by permission of James Dobson, Inc. All rights reserved.

"Special Children, Mine and God's" by Nancy Sullivan Geng from *The Catholic Digest*, September 1993, © Nancy Sullivan Geng. Used by permission of the author.

VIRTUE

"Home" by Charles R. Swindoll. Excerpted from a letter from the Oregon Center for Family Policy.

"Tough Decision" author unknown.

"The Porcelain Teacup" by Teresa Maud Sullivan (Gertrude St.

"When You Thought I Wasn't Looking" by Mary Rita Schilke Korzan © 1980. Mary's poem was inspired by her mother, Blanche Schilke. The poem is now matted and available for distribution from the author. Mary is working on her first book, a collection of original stories and poems. She resides with her husband and three children in Granger, Indiana.

GROWING UP

"Someday They Will Fly" by Erma Bombeck from *Forever Erma*, © 1996 by the estate of Erma Bombeck. Universal Press Syndicate. All rights reserved. Used by permission.

"Our Girl" by Max Lucado from *Six Hours One Friday* (Multnomah Publishers, Inc., Sisters, OR), © 1989 by Max Lucado. Used by permission.

"A Great Cup of Tea" by James Dobson from *Home with a Heart* (Tyndale House Publishers, Inc., Wheaton, IL), © 1996. Used by permission of James Dobson, Inc. All rights reserved.

"No More Oatmeal Kisses" by Erma Bombeck from *Forever Erma*, © 1996 by the estate of Erma Bombeck. Universal Press Syndicate. All rights reserved. Used by permission.

"My Two Sons" by Melody Carlson, Sisters, OR, © 1997 by Melody Carlson. Used by permission of the author.

"The Ring Bearer" by Dennis Kizziar, retold by Matt Jacobson.

"A Mother's Letter to a Son Starting Kindergarten" by Rebecca Christian, © 1997. Used by permission of the author. All rights reserved.

"Just In Case" by Tony Campolo from *What My Parents Did Right* (Tyndale House Publishing, Wheaton, IL), © 1994. Used by permission of the author.

"The Lovesick Father" by Philip Yancey from *What's So Amazing About Grace?* (Zondervan Publishing House, Grand Rapids, MI) © 1997 Philip D. Yancey. Used by permission of Zondervan Publishing House.

"He Never Missed a Game" by Robert H. Schuller from *Tough Minded Faith for Tender Hearted People* (Thomas Nelson, Nashville, TN), © 1979, 1980, 1982.

"Annie Lee's Gift" by Glenda Smithers, free-lance writer, Kingsville, MO, © 1997. Used by permission of the author.

LOVE

"Season of the Empty Nest" by Joan Mills. Reprinted with permission from the January 1981 *Reader's Digest.* © 1981 by the Reader's Digest Association, Inc.

"Love's ABC's" author unknown.

"The Mystery of Marriage" by Mike Mason from *The Mystery of Marriage* (Multnomah Publishers, Inc., Sisters, OR), © 1985. Used by permission.

"Her Hero" by Paul Harvey from *Paul Harvey's for What It's Worth* (Bantam-Doubleday-Dell Publishing, New York, NY) © 1991 by Paulynne, Inc. Used by permission.

"A Time to Dance" by Jane Kirkpatrick from *A Burden Shared* (Multnomah Publishers, Inc., Sisters, OR), © 1998 by Jane Kirkpatrick. Used by permission.

"Roses" author unknown, quoted from *More of...The Best of Bits and Pieces* (The Economics Press, Inc., Fairfield, NJ).

"Good Choice" by Liz Curtis Higgs from *Reflecting His Image* (Thomas Nelson Publishers, Nashville, TN), © 1996. Used by permission.

"A Signal at Night" by Charlotte Adelsperger, © 1997. Used by permission of the author.

"Little Red Boots" by Jeannie S. Williams, © 1997. Used by permission of the author. Jeannie S. Williams is a prolific author, lecturer and consultant in the field of education. She resides in Sikeston, MO.

MEMORIES

"Reunion" by Donna Green from *To My Daughter, with Love* (Smithmark Publishers, New York, NY), © 1993. Used by permission of Fremont & Green Ltd., Inc.

"Stories on a Headboard" by Elaine Pondant from *Home Life* magazine, August 1993. Copyright © 1993 by the Sunday School Board of the Southern Baptist Convention, Nashville, TN. Used by permission. Reprinted with permission from the March 1994 *Reader's Digest.*

"Enjoy the Ride!" by Barbara Johnson from *Joy Breaks* by Patsy Clairmont, Barbara Johnson, Marilyn Meberg and Luci Swindoll (Zondervan Publishing House, Grand Rapids, MI), © 1997 by New Life Clinics. Used by permission of Zondervan Publishing House.

GRANDPARENTS

"Picture Perfect" by Teresa Bloomingdale from *Letting Go*.

"Inheritance Day" by Philip Gulley from *Hometown Tales* (Multnomah Publishers, Inc., Sisters, OR), © 1997 by Philip Gulley. Used by permission.

"Dinner Out" by Maryann Lee Jacob, freelance writer, © 1997. Used by permission of the author.

"A Summer Smile" by Hester Tetreault, freelance writer, Warren, OR, © 1997. Used by permission of the author.

"Grandpa and Me" submitted by Jordan, age 9, to the National Center for Fathering's Father of the Year Essay Contest. Used by permission. For information call 1-800-593-3237 or visit www.fathers.com.

"Tea for Two" by Emilie Barnes from *If Teacups Could Talk* (Harvest House Publishers, Eugene, OR), © 1994. Used by permission.

"Solitude" by Erma Bombeck from *Forever Erma*, © 1996 by the estate of Erma Bombeck. Universal Press Syndicate. All rights reserved. Used by permission.

"Grandpa's Hands" by Casandra Lindell, freelance editor and writer under the company name *The Write Word*, Portland, OR. Used by permission, © 1998.

"Grandma's Laughter" by Casandra Lindell, freelance editor and writer under the company name *The Write Word*, Portland, OR. Used by permission, © 1998.

"Grandmas Make a Difference" by Betty Southard, © 1996. Used by permission.

"The Holly Trees" by Melody Carlson, freelance writer, Sisters, OR, © 1998. Used by permission of the author.

"The Gift That Kept on Giving" by Arleta Richardson from *Christmas Stories from Grandma's Attic* (Chariot Books, an imprint of David C. Cook Publishing Co., Elgin, IL), © 1991. Used by permission.

"My Baby-Sitter, Mrs. H." by Charlotte Hale, freelance writer, Savannah, GA, © 1998. Used by permission of the author.

"Stitches in Time" by Philip Gulley from *Hometown Tales* (Multnomah Publishers, Inc., Sisters, OR), © 1997 by Philip Gulley. Used by permission.

"I Love You, Grandpa!" by Clare DeLong, © 1994. Used by permission of the author. Also published in *Contents of the Weaker Vessel* and *Our Hope*. Clare is a freelance writer who lives in northern Illinois.

FAITH

"Mother's Covers" author unknown.

"Innocent Petitions" by Robin Jones Gunn from *Mothering by Heart* (Multnomah Publishers, Inc., Sisters, OR), © 1996 by Robin Jones Gunn. Used by permission.

"The Operation" from a message by Dr. Norman Vincent Peale. Copyright © 1975 by the Peale Foundation, Inc. Used by permission.

"A Bit of Eternity" author unknown.

"Jump" by Walter Wangerin Jr. from *Mourning into Dancing* (Zondervan Publishing House, Grand Rapids, MI) © 1992 by Walter Wangerin Jr. Used by permission of Zondervan Publishing House.

"Learned by Heart" by Tim Hansel from *You Gotta Keep Dancin'* (David C. Cook Publishing Co., Elgin, IL) © 1985 by Tim Hansel.

"She Went Over Her Daddy's Head" by Otto Whittaker from March 7, 1997 issue of *God's World Today* magazine (God's World Publications, Asheville, NC), © 1997. Used by permission.

"Covered with Prayer" by Linda Vogel, freelance writer, Kingwood, TX. Used by permission of the author. "Covered with Prayer" has been translated into Arabic, Hebrew, Japanese, and Spanish and given to babies around the world.

"The Perfect Spring Day" by Sandra Snavely, freelance writer, broadcaster, speaker and artist, Gresham, OR, © 1998. Used by permission.

"There's Robby!" by Ruth Bell Graham from *Legacy of a Pack Rat* (Thomas Nelson, Inc., Nashville, TN), © 1989. Used by permission of the author.

"Thoughts Midstream" by Joni Eareckson Tada from *Glorious Intruder* (Multnomah Publishers, Inc., Sisters, OR), © 1989 by Joni Eareckson Tada. Used by permission.

"I Am a Mother's Prayer" author unknown. From an Osterhus Publishing House tract. Permission granted by Osterhus Publishing House, Inc., Minneapolis, MN.

"I'll Be Back Soon" by Luis Palau from *God Is Relevant*

(Doubleday, New York, NY), © 1997 by Luis Palau. Used by permission.

"Reference Point" by Max Lucado from *The Final Week of Jesus* (Multnomah Publishers, Sisters, OR), © 1994. Used by permission.

"Homeward Journey" by Janet Paschal from *The Good Road* (Multnomah Publishers, Inc., Sisters, OR), © 1997 by Janet Paschal. Used by permission.

"Come Home!" by Billy Graham from *Unto the Hills* (Word Publishing, Nashville, TN), © 1991. Used by permission.

"First Words" by Ruth Bell Graham from *Legacy of a Pack Rat* (Thomas Nelson, Inc., Nashville, TN), © 1989. Used by permission of the author.

"Amazing Grace" by Philip Yancey from *What's So Amazing about Grace?* (Zondervan Publishing House, Grand Rapids, MI) © 1997 Philip D. Yancey. Used by permission of Zondervan Publishing House.

NOTES

"Treasure" by Strickland Gillilan.

"Honey for the Heart" by Alice Gray, © 1998. Used by permission.

"No Frigate Like a Book" by Gloria Gaither, Alexandria, IN, © 1998. Used by permission of the author. All rights retained.